SimQuick

Process Simulation with Excel

Third Edition

David Hartvigsen
Mendoza College of Business
University of Notre Dame

(Updated on 6/15/2016)

To Nancy

Table of Contents

Preface

Motivation

The simulation of processes (waiting lines, factories, supply chains, and so on) is one of the conceptually simplest and most often applied techniques in Operations Management and Management Science, yet it has not been widely taught to business students. A key reason for this is that performing process simulation requires the use of software, and the software that is available tends to be complex and expensive. Even the more graphics-based packages, although often beautifully designed, frequently have an enormous number of features that place an unnecessary burden on students (and instructors) in classes that are not devoted to simulation.

SimQuick is an Excel-based software package for process simulation that is easy to learn, easy to use, and freely distributed. (Its key features can be learned in an hour or two of class time or independent reading.) It is an ordinary Excel file with some hidden macros and should run immediately on any modern personal or networked computer that runs Excel, either a PC or an Apple computer; it is not an "add-in" and requires no "installation." Hence, users of Excel will already be familiar with much of the interface, and the results are already in the spreadsheet, ready for analysis.

SimQuick is aimed primarily at business students and managers who want to quickly learn the basics of process simulation and be able to quickly analyze and improve real-world processes. SimQuick is flexible in its modeling capability; that is, it is not a "hardwired" set of examples; it requires true modeling. The user can combine the basic building blocks of SimQuick in a huge variety of ways. Hence, SimQuick can serve well as an introduction to both the notion of building quantitative models as well as the important field of simulation. Since the first version of SimQuick was released in 2001, it has been used in industry as well as in the classroom; its original design and subsequent updates have been informed by comments from users in both domains.

This (inexpensive) booklet accompanies SimQuick. It presents the basics of process simulation by having the reader construct, run, and analyze simulations of realistic processes using SimQuick. An emphasis has been placed on explaining precisely how the various building blocks of SimQuick work. Chapter 1 contains a brief introduction to process simulation and the concepts underlying SimQuick. The next four chapters contain a variety of examples of process simulation. These examples are organized as follows: waiting lines (Chapter 2), inventory in supply chains (Chapter 3), manufacturing (Chapter 4), and project management (Chapter 5). Each example is followed by an exercise. All of the examples and exercises have been designed with business students and managers in mind.

In addition to presenting the basics of process simulation, this booklet introduces a number of *key concepts* from the analysis of processes: service level, cycle (or waiting) time, throughput, bottleneck, batch size, setup, priority rule, and so on. The booklet also introduces some *key trade-offs* from the analysis of processes: number of servers vs. service level, inventory level vs.

service level, working time variability vs. throughput, batch size vs. service level, and so on. These notions are presented through computer models that the reader constructs and experiments with using SimQuick.

How to use the booklet

The booklet is self-contained; that is, all technical terms involving processes or operations are defined. The reader is assumed to have a rudimentary understanding of how to use Excel on the level of knowing how to save files and how to enter information into cells. Also, a basic understanding of statistical distributions, such as the normal distribution, would be helpful. The chapters are organized around typical topics in Operations Management and Spreadsheet Modeling courses so that this booklet can easily be used in these types of courses.

The reader should first read Chapter 1 (which contains a conceptual explanation of process simulation and SimQuick) and Section 1 of Chapter 2 (which contains a step-by-step explanation of how to use SimQuick by completely working through a simple example). After this, the reader has a lot of freedom (with some Examples recommended as prerequisites in a few spots).

Chapters 2 through 5 consist of examples of processes that can be modeled using SimQuick. When needed, an example discusses how to build the SimQuick model. Each example is followed by an exercise.

A quick treatment of process simulation could consist of working through Example/Exercise 1 for waiting lines and Example/Exercise 19 for manufacturing. With just this material, many real-world processes can be easily modeled and studied. Adding Example/Exercise 5 with Decision Points would allow the modeling of many more types of processes. A reading of Examples 8, 9, and 10 would introduce the notion of Changing Distributions and further increase the variety of real-world processes that can be modeled. Adding Examples/Exercises 13 and 14 would provide a quick introduction to the modeling of inventory in supply chains and adding Example/Exercise 26 would serve as an introduction to the incorporation of uncertainty into project management models.

The booklet contains five appendices. Appendix 1 contains a list of the basic steps in conducting a simulation project. Appendix 2 contains tips on how to enhance SimQuick by using some of the features built into Excel. A tool with wide applicability, called Scenarios, is discussed in Appendix 3, where references are made to several Examples/Exercises from the text. Appendix 4 describes how to use a feature of SimQuick called Custom Schedules. Appendix 5 contains a succinct description of all the features of SimQuick and can be used for reference. Hence, the features of SimQuick are presented in two ways: through examples and in a reference manual.

Solutions to exercises: Instructors can obtain solutions to every exercise. To obtain solutions, an instructor should send a request to the author (Hartvigsen.1@nd.edu) with a copy of their course syllabus and a link to their webpage at their educational institution.

<u>Web site</u>: Refer to SimQuick.net for additional information on SimQuick, this booklet, and technical support.

Over the past 15 years, I have used SimQuick in the classroom with executive MBAs, full-time MBAs, and undergraduate business students. After a one-hour introduction in class (basically, covering Section 1 of Chapter 2), the students successfully solve a variety of modeling problems with little help. This introduction has also served as a launching pad for term projects, whereby students identify and analyze real-world processes of their choice.

New to the 3rd edition:

The SimQuick software and booklet have been updated in several ways in this 3rd edition. Here are the key updates:

- Due to improvements in the SimQuick software and the steady advance of computer hardware, SimQuick runs considerably more quickly than when the 2nd edition appeared. This allows more simulations to be performed in a reasonable amount of time, which leads to more accurate results. Hence, more simulations are allowed and recommended in the examples/exercises.
- A new feature called Scenarios has been added. This feature allows you to easily test, at one time, multiple variations on a given model and then compare the results in one worksheet. This feature is described in the new Appendix 3 with examples from the text.
- Another new feature called Changing Distributions allows a statistical distribution to change during the course of a simulation. With this, you can model, for example, customer arrival rates that increase and decrease during the span of a simulated day. This feature is illustrated in Example/Exercise 10, which is new to this edition.
- Models can now allow Work Stations, Entrances, and Exits to be "available" or "unavailable" during a simulation. With this feature you can more easily experiment with the number of workers or machines that are available during a simulation. This feature can also be combined with Changing Distributions to allow a worker or machine, for example, to be available during only some time periods during a simulation. This feature is illustrated in the newly added Examples/Exercises 9 and 10.
- With a new feature called Buffer Tracking you can display how inventory levels (of people or products) vary during a simulation. This allows you, for example, to pinpoint where and when bottlenecks occur, which allows, for example, more accurate adjustments of staffing levels or numbers of machines. This feature is introduced in the newly added Example/Exercise 8 and elaborated in Example/Exercise 10.
- Data entry has been simplified and streamlined with the introduction of pull-down lists within most cells of the data entry tables.
- The discussion of how to perform statistical analyses of SimQuick output (in Appendix 2) has been updated and streamlined by making use of Excel's built in statistical functions.
- You now have the option to specify a "seed" before starting a run of simulations. By doing this the same sequence of random numbers can be generated each time a group of simulations is run. (However, please note that the sequences are chosen differently on PCs and Apple machines.)

Acknowledgments

The design of SimQuick was inspired by the breakthrough simulation product XCELL, so I want to begin by acknowledging its authors: Richard Conway, William L. Maxwell, John O. McClain, and Steven L. Worona. Next, I want to thank the editor Tom Tucker at Prentice Hall, who worked with me on the first two editions. He was indispensable in helping me to define this project and bring it to fruition. I want to thank the following reviewers for their careful reading and excellent suggestions on a draft of the first edition: Sue Abdinnour-Helm, Arundhati Kumar, Larry Meile, Kelly B. Nichols, Jeffrey L. Rummel, and Billy M. Thornton. I want to thank Kristin Ann Steffeck for her copy editing on the first edition. I'd also like to thank the reviewers of the second edition for their thoughtful suggestions based on their classroom use of SimQuick: C.H. Aikens, Stephen N. Chapman, Christos Koulamas, Michael Schwartz, and Billy M. Thornton. I want to thank my colleagues Lee Krajewski and Hojung Shin for a number of helpful discussions of this project in its early stages and I want to thank my colleagues Yanjun Li, Jerry Wei, and Hong Guo for their suggestions for this third edition. I also want to thank Robert Maurer, Fazel Hayati, and Jeffery Brach for some very helpful discussions of the third edition. Finally, I want to thank my many students (executive MBAs, full-time MBAs, and undergraduate business students) of the past 15 years who have made many helpful suggestions during the development of this software and booklet. In particular, I'd like to single out Douglas Wait, Ben Gaw, Patrick Dahman, Xuejun Zhang, and Katy Delany for their insights.

Chapter 1: Introduction

Learning objectives:

- To understand the idea of process simulation.
- To understand the general structure of SimQuick models.
- To understand the role of uncertainty in process simulation.
- To get SimQuick running on your computer.

Overview

This chapter contains a brief definition of process simulation, an overview of how SimQuick works, and instructions for how to run SimQuick on a computer. Most of the details of how to use SimQuick are covered in Chapter 2, Section 1.

Section 1: What is process simulation?

Process simulation is a widely used technique for improving the efficiency of processes. Following are some examples of processes and some related efficiency problems that can be addressed with process simulation (and SimQuick):

Examples of processes:

- People moving through a bank or post office.
- Telephone calls moving through a call center.
- Parts moving along an assembly line or through a batch process or job shop.
- Inventory moving through a retail store or warehouse.
- Products moving by trucks, trains, planes, or ships through a supply chain.
- A software development project.

Examples of efficiency problems:

- How many tellers are needed to keep waiting times at a bank reasonably short?
- What effect will a new answering system have on how long customers wait at a call center?
- What effect will a new just-in-time (JIT) inventory system have on the number of units produced per day on an assembly line?
- What is the best batch size to use in a factory?
- What is the best delivery policy for goods at a warehouse?
- How much inventory should be kept on the shelves in a grocery store?
- How many machines should each worker operate in a manufacturing cell?
- How should inventory be distributed along a supply chain?
- What is the expected duration of a software development project?

With process simulation, you begin by building a computer model of a real-world process. Your initial goal is to have the computer model behave in a way similar to the real process, except much more quickly. You then try out various ideas for efficiency improvements on the computer model and use the best ideas on the real process. Thus, a lot of time and money can be saved.

Simulation is particularly useful when there is uncertainty in a process: for example, the arrival times of customers, the demand for a product, the supply of parts, the time it takes to perform the work, the quality of the work. With uncertainty, it is often difficult to predict the effects of making changes to a process, especially if there are two or more sources of uncertainty that interact.

Section 2: What does SimQuick do?

SimQuick allows you to perform process simulation within the Excel spreadsheet environment. There are three basic steps involved in using SimQuick. (For a more detailed list of steps, see Appendix 1.)

1.   Conceptually build a model of the process using the building blocks of SimQuick (introduced below).

2.   Enter this conceptual model into SimQuick. (This is done by filling in tables in a special Excel spreadsheet.)

3.   Test process improvement ideas on this computer model.

The building blocks in SimQuick are *objects*, *elements*, and *statistical distributions*. *Objects* typically represent things that move in a process: people, parts in a factory, paperwork, phone calls, e-mail messages, and so on. *Elements* typically represent things that are stationary in a process. There are five types of elements:

Entrances: This is where objects enter a process. Entrances can represent a loading dock at a warehouse, a door at a store, and so on. You must specify when objects arrive at an Entrance and in what numbers (using a statistical distribution or an explicit "custom" schedule).

Buffers: This is where objects can be stored. Buffers can represent a location in a warehouse or factory where inventory can be stored, a place where people can stand in line at a post office, a memory location in a computer for e-mail messages, and so on. You must specify how many objects a Buffer can hold.

Work Stations: This is where work is performed on objects. Work Stations can represent machines in a factory, cashiers in a store, operators at a call center, computers in a network, and so on. You must specify how long a Work Station works on an object (using a statistical distribution).

Decision Points: This is where an object goes in one of two or more (up to 10) directions. Decision Points can represent the outcome of a quality control station, different routings in the processing of a mortgage application, and so on. You must specify a rule for deciding in which direction an object goes (using a statistical distribution).

Exits: This is where objects leave a process. Exits can represent a loading dock at a warehouse, a customer buying a product at a store, and so on. You must specify when objects depart from an Exit and in what numbers (using a statistical distribution or an explicit "custom" schedule).

The third building block, *statistical distributions,* is discussed in the next section.

A SimQuick model describes how the objects move between the elements. You have a great deal of freedom in constructing models using the building blocks of SimQuick; hence, you can model a variety of real processes. Because the building blocks in SimQuick are intentionally simple, it is best suited to modeling processes of low to intermediate complexity.

When a SimQuick simulation begins, a "simulation clock" starts in the computer and runs for the designated duration of the simulation. While this clock is running, a series of *simulation events* takes place sequentially. There are three types of simulation events in SimQuick: the arrival of objects at an Entrance, the departure of objects from an Exit, and the finish of work on an object at a Work Station. Whenever an event occurs, SimQuick moves objects from element to element as much as possible. SimQuick keeps track of various statistics during the simulation (e.g., the mean inventory at each Buffer) so you can analyze what happened when the simulation is over.

Section 3: How does SimQuick incorporate uncertainty?

As in a real process, the timing of events in SimQuick can be uncertain or random. Here is an example: Suppose you are entering a model into SimQuick that contains a Work Station. You must specify how much time this Work Station works on an object. What do you do if this time varies in a random fashion at the real work station? A typical approach is to observe the real work station and record a list of real working times. Following are four common possibilities and the ways in which SimQuick models them.

Case 1: The list of real working times has a "bell-shaped" histogram:

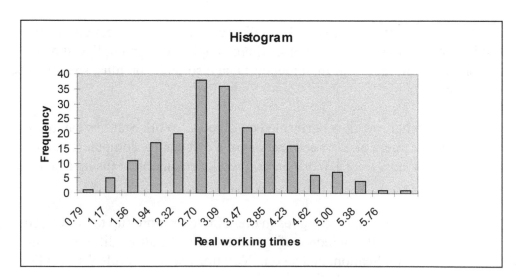

Note: The height of each bar represents the number of observed working times that fall into the interval indicated at the base of the bar on the horizontal axis.

Then, a list of numbers taken randomly from a normal distribution, with the same mean and standard deviation as your list, is likely to have a similar-looking histogram. So, for example, if your list of numbers has a mean of 3 minutes and a standard deviation of 1 minute, then you would enter Nor(3,1) into SimQuick. Thus, you are instructing SimQuick to randomly pick each working time for this Work Station from the normal distribution with mean of 3 and standard deviation of 1.

Case 2: The list of real working times has a histogram that is "skewed to the right" as follows:

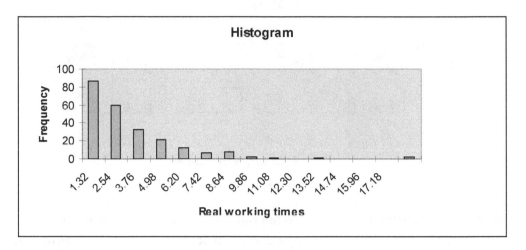

Then, a list of numbers taken randomly from an exponential distribution, with the same mean as your list, is likely to have a similar-looking histogram. So, for example, if your list of numbers has a mean of 3 minutes, then you would enter Exp(3) into SimQuick. Thus, you are instructing SimQuick to randomly pick each working time for this Work Station from the exponential distribution with mean of 3.

Case 3: The list of real working times has a histogram whose bar heights are all roughly the same:

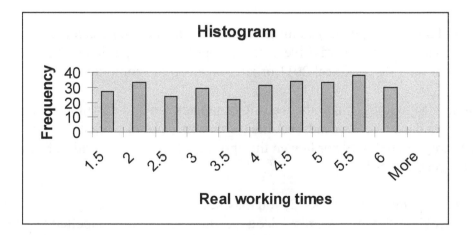

Then, a list of numbers taken randomly from a uniform distribution, with the same minimum and maximum values as your list, is likely to have a similar-looking histogram. So, for example, if your list of numbers has minimum and maximum values of 1 and 6, then you would enter Uni(1,6) into SimQuick. Thus, you are instructing SimQuick to randomly pick each working time for this Work Station from the uniform distribution with minimum and maximum values of 1 and 6.

Case 4: The list of real working times can be described by a histogram with at most ten bars:

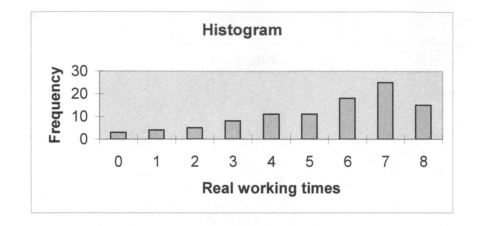

A discrete distribution in SimQuick has up to ten output numbers, each chosen with a specified probability. To model a histogram, we choose one number from each interval as an output number (as shown above) and we set its probability to be proportional to the height of its bar. Then, a list of numbers taken randomly from this output list, according to the associated probabilities, is likely to have a similar-looking histogram. In SimQuick this is modeled with the Dis function.

The details of how to use the "Nor," "Exp," "Uni," and "Dis" functions are provided in Chapters 2 through 5 and Appendix 5. To input fixed schedules, see Appendix 4.

Section 4: System requirements and "installation"

System requirements: To run SimQuick, you must be able to run Microsoft Excel on your computer. (Excel can run from your hard drive or from a network.) In particular, you need to have Excel 2003 or later on a PC, or Excel 2011 or later on an Apple computer.

"Installing" and running SimQuick: Go to the website SimQuick.net and download a copy of SimQuick-v3. It is a standard Excel spreadsheet file (with some special worksheets and macros). To use SimQuick, simply open this file or launch the application Excel and, within Excel, open the file. You are now ready to go!

Note on security: When opening SimQuick-v3, you may see "Security Warning" with a button labelled "Enable Content" or "Enable Macros." You may also see a button labelled "Enable Editing." In all such cases, just click the button. If Excel does not allow you to enable the SimQuick macros, go to SimQuick.net for some pointers.

It is probably most convenient to put a copy of SimQuick-v3 on your computer or network space and open this copy when you want to use SimQuick.

<u>Saving a SimQuick model</u>: After opening SimQuick-v3, you may save your work at any time just as you do with any Excel spreadsheet: Simply click on "Save As" under the "File" menu. You'll probably want to rename SimQuick-v3 and specify a location on your computer or network space.

If a problem arises with your copy of SimQuick-v3 (e.g., the formatting gets changed or a worksheet gets deleted), just replace it with a fresh copy from the website or your storage space.

Chapter 2: Waiting Lines

Learning objectives:

- To understand the basics of using SimQuick.
- To model, simulate, and analyze a variety of waiting line processes.
- To understand the following performance measures: service level, mean cycle (or waiting) time, and mean inventory (or number of customers in line).
- To analyze the trade-off between number of servers and service level.
- To understand the SimQuick elements: Entrances, Work Stations, Buffers, and Decision Points.
- To understand the SimQuick statistical distributions: Nor, Exp, and Dis.
- To understand the advanced SimQuick features: Buffer Tracking, the Unavailable option, Changing Distributions, Resources, and Priorities.

Overview

In this chapter, we consider waiting line processes (also called queueing systems). A typical process of this type begins with customers arriving at a service in a random fashion. They may be arriving at a bank (as in our first example), a fast-food restaurant, a car wash, or even via the phone at a 1-800 customer support center. After arriving, the customers typically get in a line, wait awhile, and then are served in some way. They may then leave the process or get in another line to be served again in another way. Management is typically interested in determining the right number of servers or adjusting the service times so that customers don't have to wait too long and so the fraction of customers able to enter the process is sufficiently high. Hence, the key performance measures of *mean cycle* (or *waiting*) *time* and *service level* are introduced in this chapter.

The first section of this chapter discusses a simple waiting line process at a bank. This section is a "must read" because it contains a thorough description of how to use SimQuick and many of its features. In particular, this section shows how to model a process with SimQuick elements, how to enter a model into SimQuick, how to run a number of simulations, and how to analyze the results. The key SimQuick elements called Entrances, Buffers, and Work Stations are introduced, as well as the statistical distributions Nor and Exp.

The second section contains examples that illustrate several other waiting line processes and associated issues that can be modeled with SimQuick. In particular, examples 2, 3, and 4 are straightforward variations of the basic bank model, involving a grocery store, a call center, and a fast-food restaurant.

The third section introduces a new SimQuick element called a Decision Point. With this element you can route objects in models in several different directions. The basics are presented in Example 5, an airport security system. Two more examples follow: a department of motor vehicles and a hospital emergency room.

The fourth section presents six additional features of SimQuick: Buffer Tracking, Unavailable elements, Changing Distributions, Discrete Distributions, Resources, and Priorities. These features greatly extend the range of real-world processes that can be modeled and help with the analysis of models. They are presented by examining variations on the bank and fast-food restaurant examples.

Section 1: Solving a problem with SimQuick

Example 1: A bank

Consider the following process within a small bank: customers enter the bank, get into a single line, are served by a teller, and finally leave the bank. Currently, this bank has one teller working from 9am to 11am. Management is concerned that the wait in line seems to be too long. Therefore, they are considering two process improvement ideas: adding an additional teller during these hours or installing a new automated check-reading machine that can help the single teller serve customers more quickly.

Modeling the process (with a process flow map)

Our first step in modeling this process is to construct a *process flow map* of the bank using the elements of SimQuick (see below). This is a conceptual step, so it can be done anywhere you prefer (e.g., on a piece of paper or on a computer). (The map below was made using some simple drawing tools within Excel; see Appendix 2 for details.) The flow map for the bank contains four elements, which are represented by boxes. For each element, the top line indicates the element type and the bottom line is a name. (We follow this convention throughout the booklet.) In this case, objects represent people and the arrows on the map indicate how the objects move between the elements. Note that the final element is a Buffer called Served Customers. An object entering this Buffer corresponds to a customer leaving the bank. This Buffer gives us an easy way to count our simulated served customers. You might have expected to see an Exit here, but with an Exit, objects leave the model according to a specified schedule instead of when they are first ready to leave. (For example, an Exit can be used to model products leaving a factory on trucks that depart periodically according to a schedule; Exits are introduced in Chapter 3.)

Process Flow Map for Bank

Entering the model into SimQuick

We're now ready to start entering our model into SimQuick.

Open your copy of the SimQuick-v3 file (see Chapter 1, Section 4, for details). You should see the following screen, which is called the Control Panel:

As with any Excel file, you can save your work at any time: simply click on "File" in the menu and then "Save As." Enter a new name (usually something to remind you of the process you are modeling) and designate a location on your computer or network space.

Observe that there are a number of buttons on the Control Panel. In particular, there is one button for each type of element. We will be clicking on these buttons to enter information for each element in our model. This can be done in any order, but let's do it in the same order in which the objects move. So click on the "Entrances" button. You should see the following screen:

For each Entrance in your model, you must fill in one table (working from left to right). So let's fill in table 1. To begin, type Door into the "Name" cell.

Note: When a cell in a table is selected, an arrow (typically) appears to the right. When you click on this arrow, a drop-down list appears. The list suggests choices for that cell (the details are discussed below). You can select something from the list to save some typing, or simply type directly into the cell. For "Name" cells and "Output destination" cells (discussed below), this list contains all the "Names" and "Output destinations" previously entered for this model.

In the next cell down, we specify when objects arrive at this Entrance. A common way to do this is by specifying the amount of time between arrivals (the so-called *interarrival time*). To do this, suppose we have spent some time observing the door of our bank and have compiled a list of actual times between customer arrivals. We discover that this list of numbers has a mean of 2 minutes and a histogram with the same shape as an exponential distribution (see Chapter 1, Section 3). (Thus, customers tend to arrive at the bank every 2 minutes, on average.) The interarrival times of customers can then be approximated by numbers, generated randomly, from an exponential distribution with a mean of 2. Thus, we enter Exp(2) in this cell. Clicking on the pull-down arrow produces a list of all the choices for this cell, including other distributions and some more-advanced features (discussed below).

General principle: Interarrival times of people at services can often be closely approximated by the exponential distribution.

In the next cell down, we specify how many objects arrive at a time. In this case, let's assume people usually arrive at the bank one at a time; thus, we enter a 1 here. (If there was uncertainty about the number of objects entering, we could enter one of our four distributions; in this case, SimQuick would round to give integers.)

Next, we specify where objects go after this Entrance. From the process flow map, we see that objects go next to the Buffer whose name is Line, so under "Output destination(s)" enter Line. (These rows should be filled in from the top down.) The table should now look as follows:

1	
Name →	Door
Time between arrivals →	Exp(2)
Num. objects per arrival →	1
Output destination(s) ↓	
Line	

Now click on "Return to Control Panel," followed by "Buffers." You should see the following screen:

Buffers	Return to Control Panel				
Examples					

	1			2	
Name →			**Name →**		
Capacity →			Capacity →		
Initial # objects →			Initial # objects →		
Output destination(s) ↓	Output group size ↓		Output destination(s) ↓	Output group size ↓	

In table 1, enter the name Line (or select it from the drop-down list). In the next cell down, we must specify the maximum number of objects that can fit into this Buffer at one time. This is a small bank, so let's say we can estimate this size as 8. So enter 8. The next cell down asks for the initial number of objects in this Buffer at the beginning of each simulation. Since the bank opens at 9am, we enter 0 here. Now we have to specify where objects go next, the "Output destination(s)"; so enter Teller here. You are also asked to specify the "Output group size." Because people leave the line one at a time, enter a 1 here. If people were leaving the line two at a time, then you would enter a 2 here. (This feature is useful when, for example, you are putting objects into batches in a factory.) The table should look as follows:

	1
Name →	Line
Capacity →	8
Initial # objects →	0
Output destination(s) ↓	Output group size ↓
Teller	1

Note: If, at some time during the simulation, an object arrives at the Entrance and the Buffer is full (i.e., it contains 8 objects), then the object does not enter the process. Furthermore, it does not enter the process later in the simulation; hence, it effectively goes away. For our bank example, this represents a customer who arrives at the bank but immediately leaves because the line is too long. (This is sometimes referred to as *balking*.)

Now, click on the "Return to Control Panel" button followed by the "Work Stations" button. You should see the following screen:

Work Stations		Return to Control Panel					

Examples

		1								**2**	
		Name →								**Name →**	
		Working time →								Working time →	
	Output destination(s) ↓	# of output objects ↓	Resource name(s) ↓	Resource # units needed ↓					Output destination(s) ↓	# of output objects ↓	

In the first table, enter the name Teller (or select it from the pull-down list). Next, we describe the "Working time" of this teller. Let's assume we have observed tellers in action for several days and discovered that their service time per customer can be approximated by numbers, generated randomly, from a normal distribution with a mean of 2.4 minutes and a standard deviation of .5 minutes. So enter Nor(2.4,.5) for the "Working time."

For "Output destination(s)," enter Served Customers. For "# of output objects," enter 1 because people leave the teller one at a time. (If, for example, this Work Station represented a machine that split objects into identical pieces, then we would enter a bigger integer.) The final two columns are not relevant for this model, so you can leave them blank. (Resources are discussed in Section 4 of this chapter.) The table should look as follows:

	1			
	Name →	Teller		
	Working time →	Nor(2.4,.5)		
Output destination(s) ↓	# of output objects ↓	Resource name(s) ↓	Resource # units needed ↓	
Served Customers	1			

Now click on the "Return to Control Panel" button followed by the "Buffers" button. In table #2, enter the name Served Customers. For the "Capacity," enter the word Unlimited (or select it from the pull-down list), which sets the capacity to a very large number that is sure to exceed the number of customers served from 9am to 11am Enter 0 as the "Initial # objects." Objects in this Buffer have no output destination, so the Buffer tables should look as follows:

1			**2**	
Name →	Line		**Name →**	Served Customers
Capacity →	8		Capacity →	Unlimited
Initial # objects →	0		Initial # objects →	0
Output destination(s) ↓	Output group size ↓		Output destination(s) ↓	Output group size ↓
Teller	1			

Click on "Return to Control Panel."

The Control Panel contains the last two cells to be filled in. "Time units per simulation" asks us for the duration of each simulation. Because each simulation represents two hours and the time units we have been using for the Entrance and Work Station already refer to minutes, enter 120 here.

General principle: A time unit in SimQuick can represent any real time interval: 1 second, 3.5 seconds, 1 minute, 1 hour, 2.5 days, and so on. However, time units must be used consistently throughout a SimQuick model (in all statistical distributions and in "Time units per simulation").

"Number of simulations" asks us for the number of times we want to simulate the 2-hour period. Because each simulation is based on randomly generated numbers, each simulation can yield different results. Hence, you typically want to do more than one simulation and to analyze the results by using means (and possibly some other statistics). Let's do 100 simulations. (In general, the number of simulations should be an integer between 1 and 10,000.) This part of the Control Panel should look as follows:

Simulation controls:	
Time units per simulation →	120
Number of simulations →	100
Run Simulation(s)	

General principle: As the amount of uncertainty in a model increases (i.e., the number of statistical distributions used and the amount of their variability), the number of simulations should increase in order to maintain a given level of accuracy in the model's outputs. Most of the models we consider in this booklet are fairly small and we do 100 simulations. (See Appendix 2 for more detail on the statistical notion of "accuracy.")

We are now ready to go, so click on the "Run Simulation(s)" button. It will probably take a few seconds (this depends on the speed of your computer). In general, it will take longer as you increase the number of elements, the time units per simulation, and the number of simulations (see Appendix 5 for limits). Some messages will appear (in the lower right portion of the Control Panel), telling you what SimQuick is doing.

If SimQuick seems to be taking too long, you may hit the Esc key at any time to abort. If SimQuick is running after 30 seconds, a window will open asking you how you want to proceed.

If you made some typing mistakes or your model violates a SimQuick rule, you will receive an error message with a pointer to where the problem occurred. You should correct the problem and then hit "Run Simulation(s)" again. A common mistake is entering an "Output destination" for an element that is not exactly the same as the "Name" of the element where you want the outputs to go. You can use the pull-down lists to avoid this problem.

Clicking the "View Model" button on the Control Panel brings up a worksheet containing copies of all the element tables defining your model. This provides a convenient way to check the logic of your model and to print it. You cannot make changes to your model on this page.

Interpreting SimQuick results

When the simulations are complete, click on the "View Results" button. You should see a table similar to the following; the exact numbers will probably be different because SimQuick generated random numbers during the simulations. Your table will have 100 numbered columns; we only display the first five here.

Simulation Results				Return to Control Panel				
Element types	Element names	Statistics	Overall Means	Simulation Numbers				
				1	2	3	4	5
Entrance(s)	Door	Objects entering process	53.88	58	56	55	57	48
		Objects unable to enter	6.70	7	3	6	18	0
		Service level	0.90	0.89	0.95	0.90	0.76	1.00
Work Station(s)	Teller	Final status	NA	Working	Working	Working	Working	Not Wor
		Final inventory (int. buff.)	0.00	0	0	0	0	0
		Mean inventory (int. buff.)	0.00	0.00	0.00	0.00	0.00	0.00
		Mean cycle time (int. buff.)	0.00	0.00	0.00	0.00	0.00	0.00
		Work cycles started	48.43	51	49	49	50	48
		Fraction time working	0.96	0.98	1.00	0.97	0.97	0.96
		Fraction time blocked	0.00	0.00	0.00	0.00	0.00	0.00
Buffer(s)	Line	Objects leaving	48.43	51	49	49	50	48
		Final inventory	5.45	7	7	6	7	0
		Minimum inventory	0.00	0	0	0	0	0
		Maximum inventory	7.77	8	8	8	8	7
		Mean inventory	4.47	5.03	4.64	3.05	6.43	3.42
		Mean cycle time	11.04	11.83	11.36	7.46	15.43	8.54
	Served Customers	Objects leaving	0.00	0	0	0	0	0
		Final inventory	47.44	50	48	48	49	48
		Minimum inventory	0.00	0	0	0	0	0
		Maximum inventory	47.44	50	48	48	49	48
		Mean inventory	22.75	22.84	24.19	22.71	23.29	22.89
		Mean cycle time	Infinite	Infinite	Infinite	Infinite	Infinite	Infinite

Although, for the most part, the meaning of these results may be obvious, it's worth discussing them in detail one time. In addition to summarizing the behavior of the model over time, the results also allow you to track down every object that was present during each simulation.

The first two columns contain the element types and names in the SimQuick model. The third column contains the types of statistics collected during the simulations. Slightly different statistics are collected for each type of element. The columns labeled 1 through 5 contain the statistics collected for the first five of the 100 simulated 2-hour time periods. Each number in the column labeled "Overall means" is the mean of the 100 numbers to its right in the complete worksheet.

For the first simulation, let's consider the element Door, which is an Entrance. We learn that 58 objects entered the model, whereas 7 were unable to enter the model. This means that during our first simulated two hours, 65 (= 58 + 7) objects arrived at the model, 58 of these entered Line, and 7 left the process (or balked) because Line was full. The *service level* is computed by SimQuick using the following formula:

$$\text{Service level} = \frac{\text{Objects entering process}}{\text{Objects entering process} + \text{Objects unable to enter}}$$

Or, in this case, for simulation 1:

$$\text{Service level} = \frac{58}{58 + 7} = .89$$

In words, the service level for each simulation is the fraction of simulated customers that arrived at the bank and were able to get in Line. More generally, this is the fraction of demand that is satisfied.

Again for the first simulation, let's next consider the element Line, which is a Buffer. First, we notice that 51 objects left the Line during the simulation and went to the Teller. We see that at the end of the simulated two hours there were 7 objects left in the Line. Observe that 51 + 7 = 58 is the number of objects that entered the model at Door. You can also read the maximum, minimum, and mean number of objects in the Line during the simulation (referred to by the general term "inventory"). Finally, we see that the "Mean cycle time" was 11.04. The *mean cycle time* of an object at a Buffer during a simulation is the mean number of time units during the simulation that an object spent in the Line. In terms of our model, this represents the mean waiting time of a person in line.

Next, let's consider the statistics collected for the element Teller, which is a Work Station:

"Final status" can be either "Working" or "Not working," and simply describes what the Work Station is doing at the end of the simulation. "Final inventory (int. buff.)" refers to a small internal buffer that Work Stations have. A Work Station has enough room to hold one object on which it has finished working. (If it outputs more than one object per work cycle, then this number of objects is the capacity of this internal buffer.) The Teller's final inventory (int. buff.) is always 0 because it can always pass finished objects to the Buffer called Served Customers. A Work Station will retain a finished object in its internal buffer when it cannot be passed to an output destination (e.g., a Buffer that is full or another Work Station that is working). If a Work Station has some objects in its internal buffer, then it cannot start working on a new object until this inventory drops to zero. Hence, a Work Station with some inventory in its internal buffer is called *blocked*.

"Mean inventory (int. buff.)" and "Mean cycle time (int. buff.)" are statistics collected for the internal buffer and are analogous to the statistics we collect for Buffers. Note that "Mean cycle time (int. buff.)" does not include the working time at the Work Station. These two statistics are equal to zero in all the simulations in this example.

"Work cycles started" indicates how many times the Work Station has begun working on an object, and "Fraction time working" indicates the fraction of the time of the entire simulation that the Work Station spent working. (This is an important performance measure that is often called *utilization* in the context of machines in a factory.) We see, for example, that the Teller is working 98% of the time during simulation 1 and all of the time during simulation 2.

"Fraction time blocked" indicates the fraction of the time of the entire simulation that the Work Station was blocked. In the bank example, the Teller is never blocked.

Interpreting the results for the Buffer called Served Customers is the same as for the Line. Note that the "Mean cycle time" is "Infinite" because no objects ever leave this Buffer.

Let's focus on those statistics that are probably of most interest to the management of this bank. These will typically be numbers in the "Overall means" column, each of which is the mean of the 100 numbers to its right in the complete spreadsheet.

At this bank, management is probably very interested in the statistic "Overall mean mean cycle time" of the Line. (Let's just refer to this as the "overall mean cycle time.") This represents the mean amount of time a customer is waiting in line. In this example, the overall mean cycle time is 11.04 time units.

A related statistic of interest is the "Overall mean cycle time" of the Line plus the Teller. This represents the mean amount of time a customer is both waiting and being served. This is easy to compute from the Results using the following formula:

Overall mean cycle time of Line plus Teller =

Overall mean cycle time of Line + Overall mean working time of Teller

Note that the overall mean working time of Teller is an input to the model; it is simply 2.4 time units (from Nor(2.4,.5)). Hence, the overall mean cycle time of the Line plus Teller equals 13.44 (= 11.04 + 2.4) time units.

Another important statistic to management is the "Overall mean service level," which represents the fraction of customers that enter the bank. In this example, the overall mean service level is .90.

Also of interest is the "Overall mean inventory." This represents the mean number of people in Line, which, in this example, is 4.47.

We can see how busy our simulated teller was by looking at the "Overall mean fraction time working," which, in this example, is .96.

A final statistic to consider is the "Overall mean final inventory" of Served Customers. This represents the total number of customers served during the simulated two hours and is sometimes referred to as the *throughput* of the process. In this example, the overall mean final inventory is 47.44.

Note: Consider any row of the Results worksheet. The number in the "Overall means" column of the Results worksheet is a summary statistic of all the numbers to its right. Another important statistical calculation with these numbers is a confidence interval, which contains the true overall mean (with a specified probability, under some reasonable assumptions). Finding a confidence interval (as well as other important statistics, like the standard deviation) is easy to do in Excel and is discussed in Appendix 2.

Note: As with the above example, we are typically most interested in the overall means column of the Results worksheet. You can prevent SimQuick from outputting the results from the individual simulations by clicking on "Other Features" on the Control Panel, and then selecting "Hide Results Details." For 50 or more simulations, this can noticeably improve the running time of SimQuick. You can specify up to 10,000 simulations for a model, but you must select "Hide Result Details" if the number of simulations exceeds 200.

Before using this model to experiment with changes in the process, management should make sure the results are close to what is observed in the real bank; this is called checking the *validity* of the model. The most important statistic to check in this case is probably the overall mean inventory or the overall mean cycle time of Line. If the model is not valid, then the structure and statistical distributions in the model need to be checked against the real process. Let's assume our model gives a good approximation of the real bank.

Improving the process, Variation 1

Let's see how much the key performance measures for this model can be reduced by adding a second teller to our model. Here is our new process flow map:

Process Flow Map for Bank, Variation 1

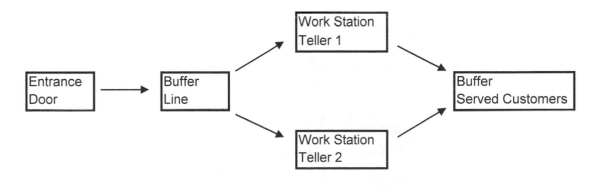

The two Work Stations operate as follows: Suppose during a simulation there is an object in Line. If Teller 1 is not working, then this object will go to Teller 1. If Teller 1 is working and Teller 2 is not working, then this object will go to Teller 2. If both Teller 1 and 2 are working, then the object remains in Line until one of them finishes.

Assume both tellers can serve customers at the same rate. Can you guess by how much the overall mean inventory and the overall mean cycle time of Line will drop from the one-teller case?

Here is the new SimQuick model (note that Line now has two output destinations):

Entrance:

1	
Name →	Door
Time between arrivals →	Exp(2)
Num. objects per arrival →	1
Output destination(s) ↓	
Line	

Buffers:

1			2		
Name →	Line		**Name →**	Served Customers	
Capacity →	8		Capacity →	Unlimited	
Initial # objects →	0		Initial # objects →	0	
Output destination(s) ↓	Output group size ↓		Output destination(s) ↓	Output group size ↓	
Teller 1	1				
Teller 2	1				

Work Stations:

1			
Name →	Teller 1		
Working time →	Nor(2.4,.5)		
Output destination(s) ↓	# of output objects ↓	Resource name(s) ↓	Resource # units needed ↓
Served Customers	1		

Name →	Teller 2		
Working time →	Nor(2.4,.5)		
Output destination(s) ↓	# of output objects ↓	Resource name(s) ↓	Resource # units needed ↓
Served Customers	1		

Here are the results from running 100 simulations with SimQuick:

Element types	Element names	Statistics	Overall Means	1	2	3	4	5
Simulation Results				Return to Control Panel				
				Simulation Numbers				
Entrance(s)	Door	Objects entering process	60.32	64	57	60	65	55
		Objects unable to enter	0.10	0	0	0	0	0
		Service level	1.00	1.00	1.00	1.00	1.00	1.00
Work Station(s)	Teller 1	Final status	NA	Working	Not Working	Working	Working	Working
		Final inventory (int. buff.)	0.00	0	0	0	0	0
		Mean inventory (int. buff.)	0.00	0.00	0.00	0.00	0.00	0.00
		Mean cycle time (int. buff.)	0.00	0.00	0.00	0.00	0.00	0.00
		Work cycles started	33.76	36	32	34	37	32
		Fraction time working	0.67	0.70	0.68	0.69	0.73	0.66
		Fraction time blocked	0.00	0.00	0.00	0.00	0.00	0.00
	Teller 2	Final status	NA	Working	Not Working	Working	Working	Not Work
		Final inventory (int. buff.)	0.00	0	0	0	0	0
		Mean inventory (int. buff.)	0.00	0.00	0.00	0.00	0.00	0.00
		Mean cycle time (int. buff.)	0.00	0.00	0.00	0.00	0.00	0.00
		Work cycles started	26.29	28	25	25	27	23
		Fraction time working	0.52	0.56	0.51	0.50	0.50	0.50
		Fraction time blocked	0.00	0.00	0.00	0.00	0.00	0.00
Buffer(s)	Line	Objects leaving	60.05	64	57	59	64	55
		Final inventory	0.27	0	0	1	1	0
		Minimum inventory	0.00	0	0	0	0	0
		Maximum inventory	3.57	7	3	5	4	4
		Mean inventory	0.37	0.82	0.45	0.39	0.36	0.58
		Mean cycle time	0.71	1.53	0.95	0.80	0.67	1.27
	Served Customers	Objects leaving	0.00	0	0	0	0	0
		Final inventory	58.93	62	57	57	62	54
		Minimum inventory	0.00	0	0	0	0	0
		Maximum inventory	58.93	62	57	57	62	54
		Mean inventory	28.85	31.69	29.35	26.27	26.52	28.97
		Mean cycle time	Infinite	Infinite	Infinite	Infinite	Infinite	Infinite

As before, a key statistic of interest is the overall mean cycle time for Line. The overall mean is now .71 time units. This is a clear improvement (and probably quite a bit better than you anticipated). We could use a t-test to prove that it is significant (see Appendix 2), but it is not necessary in this case. The overall mean cycle time of the Line plus the Tellers has decreased to .71 + 2.4 = 3.11. Observe that the overall mean service level has significantly increased to 1. Hence, all our simulated customers were able to enter the bank in each simulation. Also notice that the overall mean inventory of Line has significantly dropped to .37 objects. We see that the overall mean fraction time working of each teller (.67 and .52 time units) has dropped quite a bit. Finally, the overall mean final inventory of Served Customers, or the throughput, has increased to 58.93.

Improving the process, Variation 2

Next, let's see how much the waiting time can be reduced by installing new automated check-reading machines, instead of a second teller. The process flow map for this variation is the same as our original map with one teller. The only difference in the SimQuick tables is the working time for the Work Station called Teller. By researching the effect of installing these machines in other banks, management believes that the service time per customer can be approximated by a normal distribution with a mean of 2 minutes and a standard deviation of .5 minutes. So we enter Nor(2,.5) for the working time of Teller.

Here are the results for 100 simulations:

Simulation Results				Return to Control Panel				
Element types	Element names	Statistics	Overall Means	Simulation Numbers				
				1	2	3	4	5
Entrance(s)	Door	Objects entering process	58.07	53	56	63	64	62
		Objects unable to enter	2.39	3	0	2	3	4
		Service level	0.97	0.95	1.00	0.97	0.96	0.94
Work Station(s)	Teller	Final status	NA	Working	Working	Working	Working	Working
		Final inventory (int. buff.)	0.00	0	0	0	0	0
		Mean inventory (int. buff.)	0.00	0.00	0.00	0.00	0.00	0.00
		Mean cycle time (int. buff.)	0.00	0.00	0.00	0.00	0.00	0.00
		Work cycles started	54.30	49	56	57	57	60
		Fraction time working	0.90	0.85	0.88	0.96	0.96	0.96
		Fraction time blocked	0.00	0.00	0.00	0.00	0.00	0.00
Buffer(s)	Line	Objects leaving	54.30	49	56	57	57	60
		Final inventory	3.77	4	0	6	7	2
		Minimum inventory	0.00	0	0	0	0	0
		Maximum inventory	6.93	8	4	8	8	8
		Mean inventory	2.89	3.10	1.44	4.50	4.77	4.29
		Mean cycle time	6.21	7.60	3.08	9.48	10.03	8.59
	Served Customers	Objects leaving	0.00	0	0	0	0	0
		Final inventory	53.38	48	55	56	56	59
		Minimum inventory	0.00	0	0	0	0	0
		Maximum inventory	53.38	48	55	56	56	59
		Mean inventory	25.62	21.25	27.59	27.03	25.76	28.73
		Mean cycle time	Infinite	Infinite	Infinite	Infinite	Infinite	Infinite

Let's compare these statistics to those from our original one-teller simulation. The overall mean cycle time of Line is 6.21 time units. Again, this is a clear improvement, which can be shown to be significant with a t-test (see Appendix 2), although this seems to be unnecessary in this case. The overall mean cycle time of the Line plus the Teller is $6.21 + 2 = 8.21$, also a clear improvement. The overall mean service level has nicely increased to .97. The overall mean inventory of Line has dropped to 2.89 objects. The overall mean fraction time working of Teller has dropped a bit to .90. And finally, the overall mean final inventory of Served Customers (the throughput) has increased to 53.38 objects.

In summary, our simulations show that both improvement ideas should improve the performance of the process on all the key measures. And it appears that the first idea dominates the second on all these measures.

So what should management do? The decision now comes down to assessing the costs of the options and deciding what kind of service the bank wants to offer its customers.

Exercise 1: For each of the following models, run 100 simulations.

a.   Consider the original bank process described in Example 1, except assume the working time for each teller is approximated by a normal distribution with a mean of 3 minutes and a standard deviation of .5 minutes. Report the overall mean cycle times in Line when there are one, two, and three tellers.

b.   Consider the two-teller variation of the original model in Example 1 (with the original interarrival and working times). The bank is considering some promotions in an effort to increase the number of customers and is wondering what the effect might be on waiting times. Report the overall mean cycle times in Line as the time between arrivals goes from the present mean level of 2 minutes to 1.8, 1.6, 1.4, and 1.2 minutes (still exponentially distributed). This is an example of *sensitivity analysis*, where certain estimated inputs to a model are varied to see what effect this has on the results of the simulations. For a more efficient way to solve this problem, you can use the SimQuick feature called Scenarios, which is discussed in Appendix 3.

Section 2: Additional waiting line processes

In this section, we examine a variety of waiting line processes, which are similar to the bank example in Section 1. We consider processes based on a grocery store checkout, a call center, and a fast-food restaurant drive-thru. The restaurant example introduces how to compute the cycle time through several elements in a model.

Example 2: A grocery store checkout

Consider a grocery store between the hours of 5pm and 8pm on a weeknight. Suppose three checkout lanes are typically open, each checkout can handle customers with any number of items, and each checkout has a dedicated bagger. It has been observed that checking out (including bagging) takes a mean of 3 minutes per customer and that this is approximately normally distributed with a standard deviation of .5 minutes. The mean amount of time between customer arrivals at the checkouts is 1 minute and can be approximated by an exponential distribution. Although customers initially enter one specific line, they will move to a different line if it looks faster.

Hint: Model the three lines as a single line (or Buffer) that feeds all the checkouts. You can assume that everyone that arrives at the checkout gets into the single line, regardless of its length; thus, no one is rejected from the process. (So make sure your single line is large enough.)

Exercise 2:

a.   Draw a process flow map for your three-lane model.

For parts b to d, perform 100 simulations for each. Assume there is no one in line at the beginning of the simulations.

b.   Run the model from part a and report, for the single line, the overall mean number of customers in line and the overall mean waiting time.

c.   How much would the overall mean number of customers in line and the overall mean waiting time in line be reduced by opening a fourth checkout?

d.   The owner of the grocery store chain is considering the purchase of new bar code scanners. This would reduce the mean checkout time to 2.6 minutes (still normal), with a standard deviation of .5 minutes. For the three-lane case, what effect would this have on the overall mean number of customers in line and the overall mean waiting time in line?

Example 3: A call center

A process flow map for a call center is provided below. Here's how this process works. Customers with questions about this company's products call an 800 number. During a typical 8-hour day shift, the time between calls can be approximated by an exponential distribution with a mean of 4 minutes. The call center has 10 phone lines and hence can handle up to 10 calls at once. If a call arrives and all 10 lines are in use, then the caller gets a busy signal and has to call back later. If a call arrives and fewer than 10 lines are in use, then the call goes directly to a customer service (CS) person, if one is available, and otherwise is put on hold. The amount of time for a CS person to handle a call, once answered, can be approximated by a normal distribution, with a mean of 10 minutes and a standard deviation of 2 minutes.

Note: Because there are only 10 phone lines, the number of CS people plus the capacity of Line must be 10.

Process Flow Map for Call Center

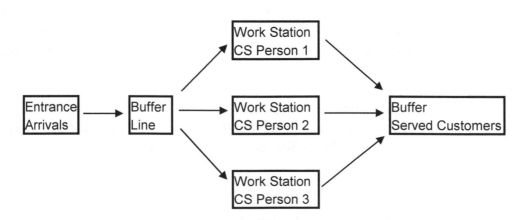

Exercise 3: Management wants to determine how many CS people to use during the day shift so that two things are both true: the mean number of minutes a person waits is less than 2 minutes

and the service level is at least .99. Consider using from one to five CS people. For each possibility, run 100 simulations of an 8-hour day shift and record the mean cycle time through Line. Assume that the initial number of callers on hold at the beginning of the day shift can be approximated by a normal distribution with a mean of 2 and a standard deviation of .5 (SimQuick will round to the nearest integer). How many CS people would you recommend for the day shift?

Example 4: A fast-food restaurant drive-thru

Management wants to study the drive-thrus at a number of Burger Queen (BQ) restaurants during the peak hours of 11am to 2pm The process works as follows. Cars arrive and line up to place an order. It's been observed that the time between car arrivals can be approximated by an exponential distribution with a mean of 2.3 minutes. There is only room for five cars to line up. The time to place an order is also roughly exponentially distributed and takes a mean of 2 minutes per car. Cars then move forward to a single window, at which they pay and pick up their order. Two cars can fit between a car placing an order and another car at the pay/pick-up window. The amount of time a car sits at the pay/pick-up window can be approximated by an exponential distribution with a mean of 2.2 minutes.

Exercise 4: For each of the following parts, perform 100 simulations. Assume that at 11am there is typically one car in line to place an order and one car in line to pay/pick up their order (so set your "Initial # objects" for your Buffers accordingly). For a process flow map of this process, see the left side of the process flow map for Example 12.

a.   Build a SimQuick model of the drive-thru, as described. Report the overall mean throughput (i.e., the overall mean final inventory in Served Cars) Also report the overall mean cycle time for the whole process. This number is the mean amount of time an object spends between entering the Buffer called Outside Order Line and leaving the Work Station called Pay/Pickup. It can be obtained by adding the overall mean cycle time through the two Buffers, the mean working time at the two Work Stations (obtained from their input distributions), and the overall mean cycle time through the internal buffer at the Work Station called Car Order. Also report the overall mean service level of the customers arriving at the process.

b.   The BQ design team is thinking about installing a faster process for making hamburgers. They believe this could reduce the time for Pay/Pickup to a mean of 1.5 minutes, again exponentially distributed. What effect would this have on the numbers reported in part a?

Section 3: Waiting line processes with Decision Points

In this section we introduce the SimQuick element called a Decision Point. This element allows us to build models where the routes for some objects are chosen randomly. The details of this element are presented in the first example, where a specified percentage of passengers going through an airport security check are randomly selected to have their carry-on bags searched.

This is followed by two more examples: a department of motor vehicles and a hospital emergency room.

Example 5: An airport security system

A process flow map for the passenger security process at one terminal of a medium sized airport is given below. The process works as follows. Between 8am and 10am, one passenger arrives every half-minute (on average, according to an exponential distribution) at the security area. Arriving passengers immediately enter a single line (with a large capacity). After waiting in line, each passenger goes through one of two inspection stations, which involves walking through a metal detector and running any carry-on baggage through a scanner. The amount of time for this inspection can be approximated by a normal distribution with a mean of 1 minute and a standard deviation of .1 minutes. After completing this inspection, 10% of the passengers are randomly selected for an additional inspection, which typically involves a more thorough search of the person's carry-on baggage. There are two stations for this additional inspection; the amount of time for it can be approximated by a normal distribution with a mean of 5 minutes and a standard deviation of 1 minute.

Process Flow Map for an Airport Security System

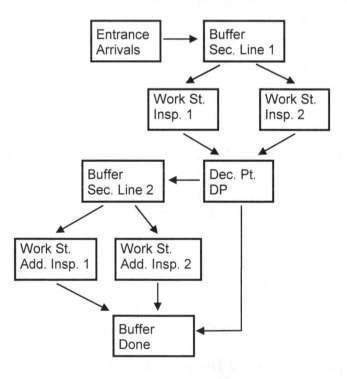

Note that this SimQuick model makes use of the Decision Point element. A Decision Point routes objects in one of several (up to ten) possible directions. In this model, the Decision Point sends each input object to either Sec. Line 2, where it awaits a second inspection, or to the Buffer called Done, for objects that have cleared security. When filling in a Decision Point table in SimQuick (see below), we must specify a rule for determining in which direction each object is sent. This rule is a probability, expressed in SimQuick as a percentage (i.e., a number between 0 and 100). In this model, there is a 10% probability that an object will be sent to Sec. Line 2 and a 90% probability it will be sent to Done. In general, the numbers in the Percents column of a Decision Point table must sum to 100.

Here are some details: A Decision Point chooses a direction for an object in zero time. However, if a Decision Point chooses a direction for an object and cannot pass the object on (e.g., the next element is a full Buffer or a working Work Station), then it will retain the object in an internal buffer (similar to a Work Station). No further objects can enter a Decision Point if there is an object in its internal buffer, hence Decision Points can be blocked (just like Work Stations). In the models in this section, blocking cannot occur because the outputs of the Decision Point are Buffers with large capacity.

General principle: In most models a blocked Decision Point is inconsistent with the real-world situation being modeled. Hence it is usually a good idea to have a Decision Point send objects to large capacity Buffers. We discuss below how to detect if blocking is occurring.

Three of the SimQuick tables for this model are given below. The capacity of each Buffer is set to Unlimited, since there is plenty of space in the airport and all passengers must pass through security. Also, the initial number of objects at each Buffer is set to 0, since demand is fairly low before 8am. We let time units correspond to minutes.

Entrance:

1	
Name →	Arrivals
Time between arrivals →	Exp(.5)
Num. objects per arrival →	1
Output destination(s) ↓	
Sec. Line 1	

Work Station:

		1	
		Name →	Insp. 1
		Working time →	Nor(1,.1)
Output destination(s) ↓	# of output objects ↓	Resource name(s) ↓	Resource # units needed ↓
DP	1		

Decision Point:

1	
Name →	DP
Output destinations ↓	Percents ↓
Sec. Line 2	10
Done	90

Here are the some of the results from 100 simulations of this 2-hour time period. (The results for the Entrance and Work Stations are not shown.)

Simulation Results				Return to Control Panel	
Element types	Element names	Statistics	Overall Means	Simulation Nui 1	2
Buffer(s)	Sec. Line 1	Objects leaving	227.37	220	231
		Final inventory	9.87	16	5
		Minimum inventory	0.00	0.00	0.00
		Maximum inventory	16.13	23.00	16.00
		Mean inventory	5.97	5.92	6.73
		Mean cycle time	3.12	3.23	3.50
	Sec. Line 2	Objects leaving	20.47	16	29
		Final inventory	0.03	0	0
		Minimum inventory	0.00	0	0
		Maximum inventory	1.63	1	3
		Mean inventory	0.10	0.02	0.27
		Mean cycle time	0.53	0.16	1.10
	Done	Objects leaving	0	0	0
		Final inventory	224.57	217	227
		Minimum inventory	0.00	0	0
		Maximum inventory	224.57	217	227
		Mean inventory	108.78	105.39	113.24
		Mean cycle time	Infinite	Infinite	Infinite
Decision Point(s)	DP	Objects leaving	225.37	218	229
		Final inventory (int. buff.)	0.00	0	0
		Mean inventory (int. buff.)	0.00	0	0
		Mean cycle time (int. buff.)	0.00	0.00	0.00

Let's consider the statistics collected for the Decision Point. First, we count the number of objects leaving it during each simulation. The overall mean from the 100 simulations is 225.37. The statistic "Final inventory (int. buff.)" is the number of objects in the Decision Point's internal buffer at the end of each simulation. This number can only be 0 or 1 for each simulation. The statistics "Mean inventory (int. buff.)" and "Mean cycle time (int. buff.)" are for the internal buffer and should be self-explanatory (they are analogous to the statistics collected for Work Stations). All of these statistics for the internal buffer are 0 for this model since the Decision Point is always able to pass objects to the large capacity Buffers that follow. If a Decision Point is blocked at any time during a simulation, then the overall means of the last two statistics should be greater than zero.

The key statistics for airport management are the passenger waiting times. From the results we immediately see that the overall mean cycle (or waiting) time for passengers is 3.12 minutes in Sec. Line 1 and .53 minutes in Sec. Line 2.

38

Exercise 5:

Management is interested in examining the effect on waiting time of increasing the percentage of passengers that undergo the second inspection. For each of the scenarios described below, do 100 simulations and report the overall mean cycle time in Sec. Line 2.

a.   Build a model of the airport security process, as described above. Consider the scenarios where the probabilities that an object will be sent to Sec. Line 2 are 10%, 15%, and 20%. This is an example of *sensitivity analysis*, where certain estimated inputs to a model are varied to see what effect this has on the results of the simulations. For a more efficient way to solve this problem, you can use the SimQuick feature called Scenarios, which is discussed in Appendix 3.

b.   Redo part a, except add a third Work Station for the second inspection.

Example 6: A Department of Motor Vehicles

A process flow map for a Department of Motor Vehicles (DMV) in a small town is provided on the following page. Here is how the process works: During the peak demand hours of 10am to 1pm, customers arrive, one at a time, at the DMV every 4 minutes (on average, according to an exponential distribution). Each customer gets into a line (with a capacity of 10 people). After waiting in line, each customer discusses what they need with a clerk. Typically, 20% of the customers want to register their car (only), 40% want to renew their licenses (only), and 40% want to do both. Those who want to do both get their license renewed first. The time of this discussion can be approximated by a normal distribution with a mean of 1 minute and a standard deviation of .1 minutes. The clerk gives each customer a number and shows them where to sit (there is plenty of room for customers to sit and wait). Observe that the Decision Point called Choice 1 separates the customers into those that only want to register their car and the rest. (It is recommended that you read Example 5 to learn about Decision Points.) A second Decision Point called Choice 2 is used to separate the people who only want a license from the people who want a license and a registration. (Be careful in setting the probabilities for these Decision Points.) The amount of time for a clerk to process a license renewal can be approximated by a normal distribution with a mean of 5 minutes and a standard deviation of .5 minutes. The amount of time for a clerk to process a registration can be approximated by a normal distribution with a mean of 6 minutes and a standard deviation of .5 minutes.

Process Flow Map for DMV

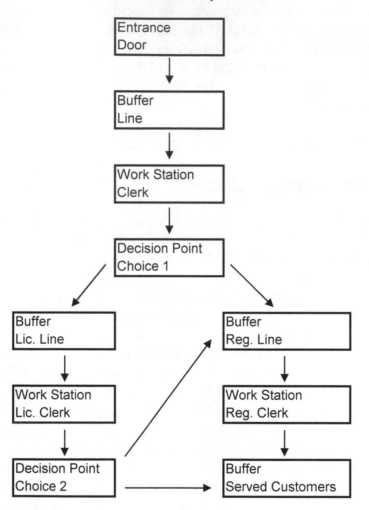

Exercise 6: Management is considering adding a new license clerk. They want to know the effect of this on the following statistic: the overall mean waiting time in the process of those customers that need both a license and a registration (i.e., the sum of overall mean cycle times in the three lines plus the mean working times of the three types of clerks). Perform 100 simulations of the present situation (for the 3-hour time period) and the situation with an additional license clerk. Report the above statistic for both cases. Also report the individual overall mean cycle times in the license and registration lines in each case. Can you explain the change in the cycle times in the individual lines? Assume there are no people in the lines at the beginning of the simulations.

Example 7: A hospital emergency room

A process flow map for a hospital emergency room is given below. (This example is closely based on an example in *Introduction to Simulation and Risk Analysis* by J. R. Evans and D. L. Olson, Prentice Hall, 1998.) To simplify the map, a number of details have been left out, hence all the boxes in the map do not directly correspond to SimQuick elements. For this model, we focus on the night shift, from midnight to 8am. During this time, patients arrive at the emergency room according to a fairly stable pattern: on average, they arrive every 15 minutes according to an exponential distribution. A patient's first stop is the check-in desk. After describing their situation to the nurse, patients are sent to one of four locations: historically, 30% are sent to the ambulatory area for immediate care, 20% are sent for x-rays, 5% are admitted directly to the hospital, and 45% are sent for lab tests. Patients finishing at the ambulatory area are all released. Of patients finishing with their x-rays, 60% are released, 10% are sent for lab work, and 30% are admitted to the hospital. Of patients finishing with their lab work, 10% are admitted to the hospital and 90% are released.

Process Flow Map for a Hospital Emergency Room

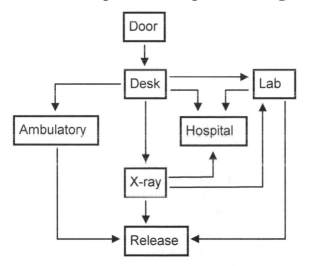

In order to build a model for this process with SimQuick elements, we must add some detail to the process map. Clearly Door is an Entrance, and Release and Hospital are large Buffers. Ambulatory represents a Buffer, followed by a single Work Station. Each of the other three boxes represents a sequence of three elements: a large Buffer, followed by a single Work Station, followed by a Decision Point. These Buffers represent waiting areas. Work Stations are, of course, where the services are performed. The working times can be approximated as follows (where we let time units represent minutes):

Work Stations	Working times
Desk	Nor(3,.1)
Ambulatory	Nor(15,6)
X-ray	Nor(15,3)
Lab	Nor(30,6)

Finally, the Decision Points route the objects to their next destination according to the observed proportions given above. (It is recommended that you read Example 5 to learn about Decision Points.)

Exercise 7:

a. Build a SimQuick model for the emergency room process. Based on historical observations, we can assume there is initially one object in the Buffer before the lab Work Station and zero objects in the other Buffers. This model has a lot of uncertainty, so do 200 simulations. (This will go faster if you click "Other Features" and "Hide Results Details"; SimQuick will then write only the overall means on the Results worksheet.) Report the overall mean fraction time working (also called the *utilization*) for each Work Station and the overall mean cycle time for each Buffer in front of a Work Station. Which Work Station is a *bottleneck* according to these statistics (i.e., has the highest values)?

b. Management wants to know the effect of doubling the capacity of the bottleneck, that is, adding an identical Work Station next to the exiting one in the model. With this additional element, rerun the model as in part a and report the same statistics. How has the bottleneck been affected?

c. Management also wants to know the effect on the original model of an increase in demand, where the time between arrivals drops to 10 minutes, on average. Rerun the model as in part a and report the same statistics. How has the bottleneck Work Station been affected?

Section 4: Advanced Features of SimQuick

In this section we consider six advanced features of SimQuick. The first feature, "Buffer Tracking," allows you to see how the inventory in a Buffer changes over the time of a simulation. The "Unavailable" feature allows disabling Entrances/Exits/Work Stations for quicker analysis of model variations. The "Changing Distributions" feature allows statistical distributions to change during the running of a simulation and, when combined with the Unavailable feature, allows random arrivals, departures and working times during specified time intervals within a simulation. The "Discrete Distribution" feature allows the input of essentially arbitrary statistical distributions into SimQuick models. These four features are illustrated in Examples 8 – 11 with variations on our original bank example.

Sometimes real-world Work Stations share a person or tool, which is in limited supply. This can be modeled in SimQuick using the feature called "Resources." The basic idea is that a Work Station cannot start working on an object unless it has all the Resources that have been assigned to it. When two Work Stations are competing for a Resource, the Work Station with higher "Priority" gets it. The Priority of a Work Station is determined by the number of the table in SimQuick into which it has been entered (the lower the number, the higher the Priority). These two features are illustrated in Example 12 with a fast-food restaurant process (as well as in Examples 20, 23, 24, and 25).

Example 8: Buffer Tracking

In some modeling situations, it is helpful to have a bit more detail about how the mean inventory level in a Buffer changes as the simulations are being run. To see how to get this information, enter the original bank model into SimQuick and then click on "Buffers" from the Control Panel. At the bottom of each table, observe that there is a "Yes – No" choice called "Buffer tracking" that you can make. The default here is "No," but you can switch this to "Yes" for any Buffer you'd like to track over time. To see how this works, enter "Yes" for both Buffers in this model. (You can type this directly or use the pull-down list.) Next, click on "Other Features" from the Control Panel and enter 50 (which is the default) into the cell labeled "Num. times to sample inventory"; this is explained below.

Rerun the model, then click on "Other Features" followed by "Buffer Tracking." You should see something like the following:

Buffer Tracking   Return to Control Panel

Column num. to graph: [ ]

	Column num.	
	1	**2**
Times	**Line**	**Served Customers**
0.0	0.00	0.00
2.4	0.36	0.09
4.9	0.64	0.77
7.3	1.00	1.50
9.8	1.37	2.31
12.2	1.60	3.15
14.7	1.86	4.09

The column labeled "Times" contains a list of 50 evenly spaced times from 0 to 120 (the number of time units per simulation). (You specified this number of times when you entered 50 into the cell labeled "Num. times to sample inventory." You can enter any integer between 10 and 200 in this cell.) Notice that to the right of the "Times" column are two more columns of numbers, each labeled with the name of a Buffer previously selected for tracking: Line and Served Customers. For each time listed in the "Times" column, each number to the right is the overall mean inventory level *at that time* for the Buffer labeling that column. (These would be grouped by Scenarios (see Appendix 3), if there were any.) For example, we see that at time 9.8 the average number of people in the Line across the 100 simulations is 1.37 and the average number of Served Customers is 2.31.

You can obtain a graph of the inventory over time for any Buffer you've tracked by entering the number of its corresponding column (see row 7) in the cell labeled "Column num. to graph." By entering 1 into this cell we get the following graph:

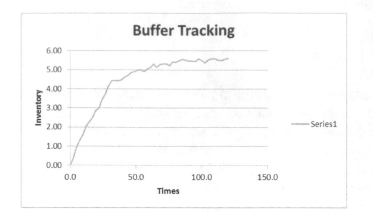

Note: Chart and axis labels are not provided in the output for the graph and were added in the standard fashion.

You can clearly see how the number of people in Line is increasing, on average, over the course of the simulations. By entering 2 into the cell "Column num. to graph" you obtain a graph of how the inventory varies during the simulations for the Buffer: Served Customers. This is the throughput for the bank and increases almost linearly during the simulations, as you'd expect.

Exercise 8: Using the 50 rows of Buffer Tracking data described in Example 8, do the following:

a. Estimate the number of people in the Buffer: Line at 10am.
b. Estimate the time between 9am and 11am at which the Buffer: Line hits 4 people.

Another application of Buffer Tracking can be found in Example 10.

Example 9: "Unavailable" elements

Sometimes it's convenient, when exploring variations on a model, to be able to make an Entrance, Exit, or Work Station "Unavailable." Here is such an example based on Example 1, the first bank model.

Suppose we are again modeling the bank from 9am to 11am. In this case the time between arrivals of customers can be approximated by an exponential distribution with a mean of 1 minute and the working time at a teller can be approximated by a normal distribution with a mean of 2 minutes and a standard deviation of .5 minutes. Let's say we want to compare our standard performance measures (overall mean service time; overall mean inventory and cycle time at Line; and overall mean final inventory at Served Customers) with one, two, and three tellers.

Enter the model, as usual, for the case of three tellers: Teller 1, Teller 2, and Teller 3. You can now run the model for this case, as usual, and record the performance. Next, in order to run the model for the two-teller case, simply replace the working time for Teller 3 with the word Unavailable, which can be typed or selected from the pull-down list for that cell (and should be capitalized). After running this model, it should be clear from the Results worksheet that Teller 3 was not used. Finally, in order to model the one-teller case, simply enter Unavailable for the working time of Teller 2 (while keeping the working time at Teller 3 as Unavailable).

A bit more time can be saved by implementing all three variations at once using the feature called Scenarios. See Appendix 3 for how to do this.

The "Unavailable" feature can also be used with the "Changing Distributions" feature, which is introduced in Example 10. In this way, for example, a Work Station can be made unavailable at certain times during a simulation. So, for example, a teller might only be on duty for 2 or 4 hours of an 8-hour work day (e.g., when customer arrivals are highest).

Finally, the "Unavailable" feature can also be used for Entrances and Exits. In these cases the word Unavailable should be entered for the time between arrivals or departures. If combined with the Changing Distributions feature, you can model, for example, arrivals or departures of parts in a manufacturing process during specific time intervals of the simulation time span.

Exercise 9: Consider the bank process described in Example 9. Using the "Unavailable" feature, run 100 simulations for each of the three cases (one, two, and three tellers) and report the overall mean service level and the cycle time in Line for each case.

Example 10: Changing Distributions

In this example, we consider another variation on the original bank example. (We will use the "Buffer Tracking" and "Unavailable" features, so it is recommended that you read Examples 8 and 9 before this one.) We want to model the entire 8-hour work day, instead of just the first two hours. A complication to doing this is that the time between arrivals at the Door has been observed to change during the course of a typical day. Also, the working time at the tellers changes during the day along with the needs of the customers. Let's approximate the changes in these two inputs by summarizing their levels every two hours as the type of customer changes. The following table models these changes based on some observations:

Time	Time between arrivals at Entrance	Working time per customer at a teller
9am – 11am	Exp(2)	Nor(2.4,.5)
11am – 1pm	Exp(1)	Nor(2.8,.5)
1pm – 3pm	Exp(3)	Nor(2,.5)
3pm – 5pm	Exp(2)	Nor(2.4,.5)

The table indicates that the arrival rates and working times from 9am – 11am and from 3pm – 5pm are the same as in the original model. However, the time between arrivals decreases (i.e., more customers) and the working time increases from 11am – 1pm; the reverse happens from 1pm – 3pm.

Let's first consider the model with a single teller. Note that the model now spans 8 hours or 480 time units (or minutes). Here are the SimQuick tables with two small changes:

Entrance:

1	
Name →	Door
Time between arrivals →	ChDist(1)
Num. objects per arrival →	1
Output destination(s) ↓	
Line	

Buffers:

1			2	
Name →	Line		**Name →**	Served Customers
Capacity →	8		Capacity →	Unlimited
Initial # objects →	0		Initial # objects →	0
Output destination(s) ↓	Output group size ↓		Output destination(s) ↓	Output group size ↓
Teller 1	1			

Work Stations:

1			
	Name →	Teller 1	
	Working time →	ChDist(2)	
Output destination(s) ↓	# of output objects ↓	Resource name(s) ↓	Resource # units needed ↓
Served Customers	1		

Notice that the time between arrivals at the Door is now ChDist(1) and the working time at Teller 1 is now ChDist(2). This instructs SimQuick to use the distributions described by tables 1 and 2 that can be viewed by clicking on "Other Features" on the Control Panel and then "Changing Distributions." The tables are filled in as follows:

Changing Distributions Return to Control Panel

Up to 50 different distributions can be entered in each table.

1			2	
Times ↓	Distributions ↓		Times ↓	Distributions ↓
0	Exp(2)		0	Nor(2.4,.5)
120	Exp(1)		120	Nor(2.8,.5)
240	Exp(3)		240	Nor(2,.5)
360	Exp(2)		360	Nor(2.4,.5)

Observe that table 1 lists times in the left column based on minutes, which are the time units of the simulations. Hence at time 0 (the start of each simulation), the time between arrivals at Door is given by Exp(2). At time 120 it switches to Exp(1), and at time 240 it switches to Exp(3). At time 360 it switches back to Exp(2) and, since this is the last filled-in row in the table, the model uses this distribution until the simulation ends at time 480. Table 2 similarly describes how the working times for Teller 1 change during a simulation.

Before running this model (let's say for 100 simulations), check "Yes" for Buffer Tracking for the Line and, on the "Other Features" worksheet, input 50 for the "Number of times to sample inventory."

Looking at the Results worksheet for one run of 100 simulations of the model, we see that the service level is .68, the overall mean inventory for Line is 4.58, and the overall mean cycle time for Line is 11.94. These numbers are not great, but they don't tell the whole story, since the arrival and working times vary. So let's go to "Other Features" and "Buffer Tracking" to obtain the following graph of how the inventory varied across our simulations:

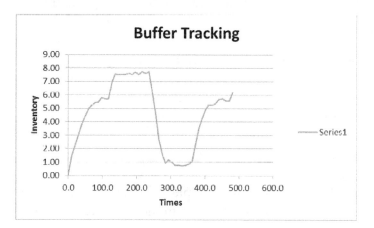

Note: Labels were added later in the standard fashion.

Not surprisingly, the inventory increases steadily from 9am – 11am (as in the original model), is almost at capacity from 11am – 1pm, drops quite a bit from 1pm – 3pm, and starts increasing again from 3pm – 5pm.

There are several options that we might consider if we want to bring the inventory levels down:

1. Add a second teller from 11am – 1pm.
2. Add a second teller for the full 8 hours.
3. Add a second teller for the full 8 hours with a third teller from 11am – 1pm.
4. Add a second and third teller for the full 8 hours.

Options 2 and 4 are straightforward to implement. Options 1 and 3 require the use of a third Changing Distribution entered into table 3 as follows:

Changing Distributions   Return to Control Panel   Return to Other Features

Up to 50 different distributions can be entered in each table.

1			2			3	
Times ↓	Distributions ↓		Times ↓	Distributions ↓		Times ↓	Distributions ↓
0	Exp(2)		0	Nor(2.4,.5)		0	Unavailable
120	Exp(1)		120	Nor(2.8,.5)		120	Nor(2.8,.5)
240	Exp(3)		240	Nor(2,.5)		240	Unavailable
360	Exp(2)		360	Nor(2.4,.5)			

Observe that the Changing Distribution in table 3, when assigned to a Work Station, has a teller working only from time 120 to time 240, as desired, by making use of the "Unavailable" feature at all other times.

See Appendix 3 for how to run the original model in this example and the four variations all at one time using Scenarios.

Exercise 10: Run the original model described in Example 10 and then the four options, each for 100 simulations. For all five models, report the overall mean service levels at Door, and the overall mean inventories and overall mean cycle times for Line. Also report the Buffer Tracking charts. Compare the solutions.

Example 11: Discrete Distributions

Let us reconsider the one-teller process in Example 1; in particular, we keep the same four-element process flow map. The only difference is in the working time of Teller.

Suppose we have observed a real teller between 9am and 11am and collected 80 representative service times. These data are summarized by the following table and histogram:

Interval (minutes)	Frequency	Relative frequency
1-2	15	19%
2-3	5	6%
3-4	25	31%
4-5	30	38%
5-6	5	6%

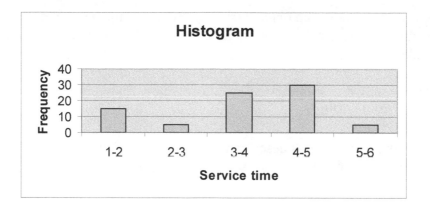

Histogram

The table tells us that 15 observed service times were between 1 and 2 minutes, 5 were between 2 and 3 minutes, and so on. The relative frequency is just the frequency divided by 80 (and rounded). The histogram is simply a graphical display of the data in the first two columns of the table. It appears from the histogram that this data does not follow one of the three built-in SimQuick distributions: normal, exponential, or uniform (see Chapter 1, Section 3). We next describe how this distribution can be approximated using the discrete distribution option within SimQuick.

Click the "Other Features" button on the Control Panel and then click the "Discrete Distributions" button. Fill in the first table as follows:

1	
Values ↓	Percents ↓
1.5	19
2.5	6
3.5	31
4.5	38
5.5	6

The numbers in the "Values" column are the midpoints of the intervals in the summary of our collected data; the numbers in the "Percents" column are the associated relative frequencies (these numbers must sum to 100, so, in general, they may have to be adjusted a bit). Hence a reasonably long sequence of numbers chosen randomly from the Values column according to the probabilities in the Percents column should have a histogram that looks like the histogram above, and hence should be a reasonable approximation for the distribution of teller service times that we observed.

We instruct SimQuick to use this distribution by filling in the table for Teller as follows:

1			
Name →	Teller		
Working time →	Dis(1)		
Output destination(s) ↓	# of output objects ↓	Resource name(s) ↓	Resource # units needed ↓
Served Customers	1		

What happens now is that whenever an object arrives at Teller during a simulation, the working time is chosen according to discrete distribution table 1 (hence the number in parentheses after "Dis" is always a table number).

In general, any distribution that is summarized by a histogram with ten or fewer bars, can be approximated by a discrete distribution in SimQuick.

Exercise 11: Consider the bank process described in Example 11. Run 100 simulations and report the overall mean service levels and the cycle times in Line when there are one, two, and three tellers.

Example 12: Resources and Priorities

Consider the BQ restaurant described in Exercise 4, part b. (You don't need to work Exercise 4 in order to do Exercise 12 below.) The BQ design team is considering the possibility of cross-training the worker assigned to the pay/pick-up window, whose working time at Pay/Pickup can be approximated by an exponential distribution with a mean of 1.5 minutes. Thus, if no one is at the pay/pick-up window, this person would serve a walk-in customer. The process flow map is provided below.

Process Flow Map for a Cross-Trained Worker at a Fast-Food Restaurant

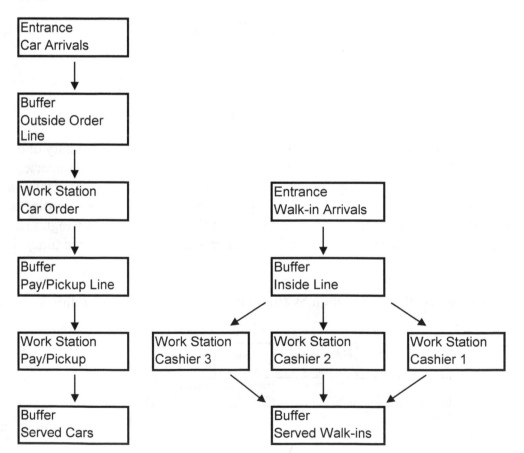

Note that this process has two Entrances, one for cars at the drive-thru and one for people entering the restaurant. We want this process to work in the usual fashion, except that only one (cross-trained) person is operating both Work Stations Pay/Pickup and Cashier 3. In particular, if there is a customer in the Pay/Pickup Line, then the cross-trained person should serve this customer next. However, if there is no customer in the Pay/Pickup Line, if both Cashier 1 and Cashier 2 are serving customers, and if there is a customer in the Inside Line, then the cross-trained person should serve this customer at the Work Station called Cashier 3. (Of course, once the cross-trained person starts serving an inside customer, he or she should finish serving this customer before going back to serve a drive-thru customer that may have arrived at the window.)

Here are the additional details for this example: The time between the arrivals of walk-ins can be approximated by an exponential distribution with a mean of 2 minutes. The Inside Line can hold about 15 people. The amount of time for a cashier to serve a customer can be approximated by a normal distribution with a mean of 4.1 minutes and a standard deviation of .5 minutes. The details for the drive-thru are the same as for Exercise 4, part b.

This situation can be modeled with SimQuick using "Resources" and "Priorities." To implement this, begin by filling in the SimQuick tables as usual. Next, click on the "Other Features" button on the Control Panel, followed by the "Resources" button, and fill in the table as follows:

Name ↓	Number available ↓
CT Worker	1

CT Worker represents our cross-trained worker and 1 means we have one such resource available. Next we assign this resource to the two Work Stations that need it to work: Pay/Pickup and Cashier 3. The Work Station tables are filled in as follows:

1			
Name →	Car Order		
Working time →	Exp(2)		
Output destination(s) ↓	# of output objects ↓	Resource name(s) ↓	Resource # units needed ↓
Pay/Pickup Line	1		

2			
Name →	Pay/Pickup		
Working time →	Exp(1.5)		
Output destination(s) ↓	# of output objects ↓	Resource name(s) ↓	Resource # units needed ↓
Served Cars	1	CT Worker	1

3		
Name →	Cashier 1	
Working time →	Nor(4.1,.5)	
Output destination(s) ↓	# of output objects ↓	Resource name(s) ↓	Resource # units needed ↓
Served Walk-ins	1		

4		
Name →	Cashier 2	
Working time →	Nor(4.1,.5)	
Output destination(s) ↓	# of output objects ↓	Resource name(s) ↓	Resource # units needed ↓
Served Walk-ins	1		

5		
Name →	Cashier 3	
Working time →	Nor(4.1,.5)	
Output destination(s) ↓	# of output objects ↓	Resource name(s) ↓	Resource # units needed ↓
Served Walk-ins	1	CT Worker	1

The 1 under "Resource # units needed" means that Pay/Pickup and Cashier 3 need one unit of CT Worker to work. Because we have only 1 such unit available, only one of these two Work Stations can work at the same time. In general, in order to work, a Work Station with a resource must have one of each of its inputs, must not be blocked, and must acquire the prescribed number of each resource that has been assigned to it. Once a Work Station has acquired a resource, it retains that resource until it's finished working. At that time, the resource becomes available to any Work Station that requires it and is ready to go.

The final issue is priority. This is determined by the number of the table into which the Work Stations have been entered (the lower the table number, the higher the priority). For this example, Cashiers 1 and 2 have priority over Cashier 3 (i.e., they will take customers from Inside Line before Cashier 3 does). Also, Pay/Pickup has priority over Cashier 3: If CT Worker is not working and there are customers in both Pay/Pickup Line and Inside Line, then CT Worker will go to Pay/Pickup and serve the drive-thru customer.

Exercise 12:

a.   Run 100 simulations of the model (from 11am to 2pm) assuming there is no cross-trained worker (i.e., there is no Work Station called Cashier 3 and there is no cross-trained worker; hence, there is a worker exclusively working at Pay/Pickup and it's not necessary to use any resources). Assume that at 11am there is typically one car in line to place an order, one car in line to pay/pick up their order, and two people in line inside the restaurant. Report the overall mean cycle time in the Inside Line, the overall mean cycle time for the whole drive-thru process (this is defined in Exercise 4), the service levels both inside and outside, and the fraction time working of Pay/Pickup.

b.   Run 100 simulations of the model with the cross-trained worker. Report the same numbers as in part a. Also report the "mean number in use" for the resource CT Worker (this can be found at the bottom of the Results page). This represents the fraction of time the cross-trained worker is working and should be equal to the sum of the fraction time working of Pay/Pickup and Cashier 3.

Chapter 3: Inventory in Supply Chains

Learning objectives:

- To model, simulate, and analyze three inventory policies widely used in supply chains: the periodic review, reorder point, and base stock policies.
- To understand the following performance measures: service level, customer waiting time, ordering cost, and holding cost.
- To understand the trade-offs between: order size, reorder point, service level, customer waiting time, lead time, ordering cost, and holding cost.
- To understand the SimQuick element called an Exit.

Overview

In this chapter, we address the basic question of inventory management: How much and when to order? We do this mainly for retail stores. However, one example considers a warehouse and one example considers a warehouse and two stores in a multi-tiered supply chain. The examples are arranged in increasing order of modeling complexity.

We look at two simple and widely used inventory policies: the *periodic review* and the *reorder point* policies. In a periodic review policy, orders are placed by the store at predetermined times (say, once a week) and the size of the order varies. The first example (Example 13), in a grocery store, is a simple illustration of this policy and the final example (Example 18), in a department store, is a more complex illustration. In a reorder point policy, orders are placed by the store when the inventory decreases to a predetermined level; the size of the order is fixed. Examples 14–16 are of this type. Example 17 is a slight variant of this; it illustrates what's called a *base stock policy*, where orders are placed by the store whenever the inventory decreases by a prescribed amount. Each policy has advantages and disadvantages and situations in which it works best.

A key performance measure (except in Example 17, an appliance store application) is the *service level* of the customer, which is the fraction of demand that is satisfied. The corresponding measure in the appliance store is the amount of time customers must wait for their purchases to be delivered to them. Another key performance measure (except in the first example) is *inventory cost*: *ordering cost* plus *holding cost*. Several examples illustrate the fundamental trade-off between these two costs. (The ordering cost is the cost to place an order; it is considered to be independent of the size of the order and hence consists mainly of the cost of preparing an order, but may also include, for example, transportation costs. The holding cost is the cost of holding one item in inventory for some period of time; a major component of the holding cost is the cost of having money tied up in inventory.)

A new SimQuick element called an Exit is introduced in this chapter. The details are covered in the first example. Exits are used to model customer demand and are quite similar to the Entrances, which were introduced in the previous chapter. In the last two examples, customer demand is modeled instead with an Entrance and two or three additional elements. Using Entrances in this way allows the modeling of more complex situations: backlogged orders and a general periodic review policy.

Inventory problems of the type we consider are often addressed using standard formulas instead of simulation. An advantage of using process simulation is that you are not limited to the assumptions underlying the formulas. In particular, with simulation you have more freedom in describing the statistical properties and the detailed workings of the process. A disadvantage of using simulation for inventory problems (and for "optimization" problems, in general) is that you may have to perform a large number of simulations to find a good solution; and this solution is not guaranteed to be optimal.

The exercises in this section require the reader to run a basic model multiple times with only small changes. Using the SimQuick feature called *Scenarios* can ease this work. This is described in Appendix 3.

The sections in this chapter build on one another and should be read in sequence.

Section 1: A periodic review inventory policy

Example 13: Grocery store inventory

Management at a grocery store has received some complaints from customers that the store occasionally runs out of SuperWheat bread, which is baked by the SuperBread Company. Here is how the inventory process presently works.

A truck from the SuperBread bakery drops off several types of loaves of freshly baked bread at the grocery store every other day. For each type of bread from the bakery, there is designated space on the shelves of the store and in the back of the store (the total space allotted to each type of bread depends on the demand for that type of bread). The driver drops off enough loaves of each type so the designated space for each type of bread is filled. The store has designated enough space to hold 70 loaves of SuperWheat bread. An examination of sales records (at times when there is SuperWheat on the shelf) shows that the time between purchases of a loaf of SuperWheat is .3 hours on average (with an exponential distribution). The store is open 12 hours per day, 7 days per week.

Management wants to determine the amount of storage space that should be designated for SuperWheat bread so that 99% of the customer demand is satisfied. Management is also curious to know, on average, how long a loaf of SuperWheat bread is in the store.

Modeling the process with SimQuick

This process can be modeled with three elements. A process flow map and the three SimQuick tables are provided below. For this model, time units represent hours that the store is open and objects represent loaves of SuperWheat.

Process Flow Map for Grocery Store Inventory

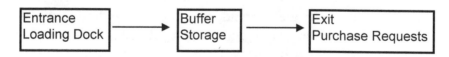

Entrance:

1	
Name →	Loading Dock
Time between arrivals →	24
Num. objects per arrival →	200
Output destination(s) ↓	
Storage	

Buffer:

1	
Name →	Storage
Capacity →	70
Initial # objects →	0
Output destination(s) ↓	Output group size ↓
Purchase Requests	1

Exit:

1	
Name →	Purchase Requests
Time between departures →	Exp(.3)
Num. objects per departure ›	1

The arrivals of SuperWheat at the store are modeled by an Entrance with the name Loading Dock. The time between arrivals is 24, which is the number of working hours in two days at the store. The "Number of objects per arrival" is 200, which is an arbitrary large number; it simply means the delivery truck carries lots of bread and can easily supply the store with as much bread as needed on each delivery. Because the time between arrivals is a constant, SimQuick will begin each simulation with an arrival at this Entrance.

The storage space for SuperWheat at the store (space on the shelf plus space in the back of the store) is modeled by a Buffer with the name Storage. When a shipment of objects (loaves) arrives, as much as will fit is moved into this Buffer (objects in the shipment that don't fit are simply taken away and cannot return at a later time (who wants old bread?)). Note that at the beginning of each simulation this Buffer is empty; however, it will immediately fill up because, as noted above, each simulation begins with an arrival at the Entrance.

Loaves are removed from store inventory when a customer makes a "purchase request" and there is a loaf in inventory. Purchase requests are modeled by an Exit called Purchase Requests. Note that for an Exit we must specify the time between departures. In our model, this represents the time between purchase requests, which we have observed can be modeled by an exponential distribution with a mean of .3 hours. As with the bank example, the distribution of time between arrivals of people at services (and hence the time between their purchase requests) is typically exponential. The "Number of objects per departure" is 1 (since our exponential distribution is based on the average time between sales of single loaves; for different applications, we could enter one of our statistical distributions here). If during the simulation a purchase request occurs, but there is no object in Storage, then this is a lost sale (also called a *stockout*). SimQuick will keep track of these. (In general, if the "Num. of objects per departure" is bigger than 1, then this number of objects (or as many as are available) is removed from the process.)

Management estimates that this demand pattern should be the same for the next 30 working days, so let's set the "Time units per simulation" to be 360 (= (30 days) * (12 hours/day)) and let's run 100 simulations.

Interpreting SimQuick results

Here is what happened during one run of 100 simulations:

Simulation Results			Return to Control					
Element types	Element names	Statistics	Overall Means	Simulation Numbers				
				1	2	3	4	5
Entrance(s)	Loading Dock	Objects entering process	1042.44	1049	1050	1039	1043	1045
		Objects unable to enter	1957.56	1951	1950	1961	1957	1955
		Service level	0.35	0.35	0.35	0.35	0.35	0.35
Buffer(s)	Storage	Objects leaving	1041.76	1049	1050	1039	1039	1045
		Final inventory	0.68	0	0	0	4	0
		Minimum inventory	0.00	0	0	0	0	0
		Maximum inventory	70.00	70	70	70	70	70
		Mean inventory	30.93	31.04	29.37	30.17	31.68	31.73
		Mean cycle time	10.69	10.65	10.07	10.45	10.98	10.93
Exit(s)	Purchase Requests	Objects leaving process	1041.76	1049	1050	1039	1039	1045
		Object departures missed	159.81	153	165	161	160	148
		Service level	0.87	0.87	0.86	0.87	0.87	0.88

Let's consider the results for the Exit: Purchase Requests. In the first simulation, the number 1049 refers to the number of simulated loaves purchased. The number 153 refers to the number of simulated purchase requests that were not filled (i.e., the number of lost sales). Hence, for each simulation, the total demand during the 30 simulated days is given by:

Objects leaving process + Object departures missed

The *service level* for each simulation is defined to be the fraction of demand that is satisfied; it is calculated as follows:

$$\text{Service level} = \frac{\text{Objects leaving process}}{\text{Objects leaving process} + \text{Object departures missed}}$$

Hence, for the first simulation,

$$\text{Service level} = \frac{1049}{1049 + 153} = .87$$

A reasonable measure of the service level of the process is the overall mean of the service levels calculated for each simulation. This is also calculated by SimQuick in the fourth column. In this example, it is equal to .87.

Note that the overall mean cycle time at Storage gives us an estimate of how long loaves of SuperWheat sit in inventory at the store before being purchased (in this case, 10.69 hours of working time).

Exercise 13:

a.   Vary the "Capacity" of Storage from 70 to 94 in increments of 4. For each capacity level, perform 100 simulations and report the overall mean service level for Purchase Requests. (Recall that we assume the bakery has adequate capacity to supply these various amounts to the store because we have set "Number of objects per arrival" to 200.) Also report the overall mean cycle time of simulated loaves in Storage. What level of inventory do you recommend to achieve a service level of .95?

b.   Store management is considering having the bakery make deliveries every day instead of every other day. This will allow the store to reduce the shelf space dedicated to SuperWheat (and other products from this bakery) and thereby offer some additional products to the customers. For this variation, vary the "Capacity" of Storage from 34 to 54 in increments of 4. For each capacity level, perform 100 simulations and report the overall mean service level for Purchase Requests. Also report the overall mean cycle time of simulated loaves in Storage. What level of inventory do you recommend to achieve a service level of .95?

If you like, see Appendix 3 for how to use the feature Scenarios to run these model variations more efficiently.

Section 2: Reorder point inventory policies

In this section, we illustrate the reorder point inventory policy by considering two examples: an electronics superstore and a warehouse.

Example 14: An electronics superstore

A large electronics superstore sells a popular handheld computer. The store presently manages its inventory of this item with the following process: When the number of computers in stock drops to 20, it places an order for 35 to the manufacturer. (20 is called the *reorder point* and 35 is called the *order size*.) The amount of time to receive an order varies a bit, but can be approximated by a normal distribution with a mean of 5 days and a standard deviation of .3 days.

An examination of sales records (at times when there are computers in stock) shows that the time between purchases of a computer is 2 hours on average (with an exponential distribution). The store is open 10 hours per day, 7 days per week. The store estimates that during the next 2 months this demand pattern should remain steady.

Management wants to satisfy at least 90% of the customer demand directly from the store's inventory. Subject to this, of course, management wants to minimize its costs. In this case, the costs are $100 every time an order is placed (regardless of its size) and $.50 per day for every computer that is in inventory at the store. Management wants to determine whether it should change its reorder point and order size.

Modeling the process with SimQuick

The inventory process used by this store can be modeled in SimQuick using four elements. A process flow map and the SimQuick tables are provided below. For this model, time units represent hours and, of course, objects represent computers.

Process Flow Map for an Electronics Superstore

Buffers:

1			2	
Name →	Factory		**Name →**	Reorder Point
Capacity →	1000		Capacity →	20
Initial # objects →	1000		Initial # objects →	20
Output destination(s) ↓	Output group size ↓		Output destination(s) ↓	Output group size ↓
Delivery	35		Purchase Requests	1

Work Station:

1				
	Name →	Delivery		
	Working time →	Nor(50,3)		
Output destination(s) ↓	# of output objects ↓	Resource name(s) ↓	Resource # units needed ↓
Reorder Point	35		

60

Exit:

	1
Name →	Purchase Requests
Time between departures →	Exp(2)
Num. objects per departure →	1

The Exit called Purchase Requests models customer demand. Based on our observations of past sales, we enter Exp(2) for the time between departures of the Exit. Since this estimate of time between departures is based on sales of single computers, we enter 1 for the "Number of objects per departure."

Store inventory is modeled by objects in two locations in our SimQuick model: the Buffer called Reorder Point and the internal buffer of the Work Station called Delivery.

Recall: Every Work Station has an internal buffer that can hold the objects completed after one working cycle. As long as there are objects in this buffer, the Work Station cannot start working on a new object and it is called *blocked*.

As this model runs, the Exit pulls objects from Reorder Point, and Reorder Point pulls objects from the internal buffer of Delivery. Consider what happens when the number of objects in the internal buffer hits zero. At this time, the inventory in our simulated store is entirely contained in the Reorder Point Buffer; hence, the amount of inventory is less than or equal to the reorder point of 20 (which is the capacity of Reorder Point). Also, at this time, Delivery becomes unblocked and pulls an object from Factory and begins working on it. This corresponds to placing an order. Note that the working time of Delivery is the delivery time from the factory: Nor(50,3) because there are 10 working hours per day. When Delivery finishes working, it deposits 35 objects into its internal buffer (35 is the "Number of output objects" for Delivery, which is the order size). As many of these objects as possible are passed to Reorder Point, where they become available to our simulated customers. Delivery is blocked until it can pass all its inventory to Reorder Point (at which point another simulated order is placed).

Note that the "Output group size" of the Buffer called Factory is equal to 35. This means that every time Delivery obtains one object from Factory, the number of objects in Factory drops by 35. Also note that the "Initial # objects" of the Buffer called Reorder Point is 20. Thus, each simulation begins with the placement of an order.

Because the demand pattern is expected to remain stable for two months, the number of time units per simulation should be 600 (= (2 months)*(30 days per month)*(10 hours per day)).

Below is some of the output from 100 simulations of the present inventory policy.

Element types	Element names	Statistics	Overall Means	Simulation Numbers 1	2	3	4	5
Simulation Results				**Return to Control Panel**				
Work Station(s)	Delivery	Final status	NA	Not Working	Working	Working	Working	Working
		Final inventory (int. buff.)	2.46	6	0	0	0	0
		Mean inventory (int. buff.)	3.06	3.99	2.94	2.95	3.13	2.60
		Mean cycle time (int. buff.)	7.33	10.02	7.19	7.23	7.66	5.58
		Work cycles started	7.95	7	8	8	8	9
		Fraction time working	0.64	0.60	0.65	0.63	0.62	0.68
		Fraction time blocked	0.36	0.40	0.35	0.37	0.38	0.32
Buffer(s)	Factory	Objects leaving	278.25	245	280	280	280	315
		Final inventory	721.75	755	720	720	720	685
		Minimum inventory	721.75	755	720	720	720	685
		Maximum inventory	1000.00	1000	1000	1000	1000	1000
		Mean inventory	851.80	862.75	848.22	849.68	852.34	839.46
		Mean cycle time	1841.03	2112.86	1817.61	1820.74	1826.43	1598.98
	Reorder Point	Objects leaving	260.28	239	259	251	251	283
		Final inventory	11.01	20	6	14	14	17
		Minimum inventory	0.00	0	0	0	0	0
		Maximum inventory	20.00	20	20	20	20	20
		Mean inventory	12.75	13.37	12.83	12.79	12.86	11.27
		Mean cycle time	29.48	33.56	29.73	30.57	30.75	23.90
Exit(s)	Purchase Requests	Objects leaving process	260.28	239	259	251	251	283
		Object departures missed	38.70	44	37	40	46	65
		Service level	0.87	0.84	0.88	0.86	0.85	0.81

Observe that the overall mean service level of .87 is below management's goal of satisfying 90% of the customer demand. Service level is most directly affected by the reorder point in the inventory policy. Hence, it appears that the present reorder point of 20 must be increased.

Next, let's consider how to calculate the cost of this inventory policy. First, the store pays $100 for every order it places. The mean number of orders placed in our simulations is the overall mean number of work cycles started at the Work Station called Delivery (7.95 in this case). Hence, we may estimate the store's ordering cost during the simulations to be ($100 per order)*(7.95 orders) = $795. The store also pays $.50 per day for every computer that is in inventory at the store. The overall mean number of computers in inventory is the sum of the overall mean number in the internal buffer of Delivery plus the overall mean number in Reorder Point. Hence, we may estimate the store's holding cost during the simulations to be (60 days)*($.50 per day per computer)*(3.06 + 12.75 computers) = $474.30. So the total cost is $795.00 + $474.30 = $1269.30.

Finally, it's easy to estimate the overall mean amount of time that a computer sits in inventory at the store. It's given by the overall mean cycle time of the internal buffer of Delivery plus the overall mean cycle time of Reorder Point. In this case, we get 7.33 + 29.48 = 36.81 hours.

Management has decided to consider a number of different scenarios in looking for a solution to their inventory problem. These scenarios are summarized by the rows in the following table.

Order Size	Reorder Point
35	25
45	25
55	25
65	25
75	25

Exercise 14: For each scenario in the previous table, run 100 simulations and report the overall mean service level and the estimated total cost. Does this new reorder point achieve the desired service level of .9? If so, which scenario would you recommend? As the order size increases, what happens to the ordering and holding costs? (If you like, see Appendix 3 for how to use the feature Scenarios to run these model variations more efficiently.)

Example 15: A warehouse

A warehouse temporarily holds printers for a chain of computer stores. Trucks from the stores arrive periodically to pick up printers. Exactly when pick-ups occur and how many printers are picked up is uncertain because it depends on the demand at the stores. The time between the arrival of each truck can be approximated by an exponential distribution with a mean of 2 days. The number of printers that are requested at each pick-up can be approximated by a normal distribution with a mean of 12 and a standard deviation of 1. The time to receive an order from the factory can be approximated by a normal distribution with a mean of 7 days and a standard deviation of 1 day. The warehouse wants to satisfy at least 90% of the demand from the stores. The warehouse is considering the reorder point scenarios (rows) in the following table.

Order Size	Reorder Point
80	50
120	50
160	50
200	50
80	60
120	60
160	60
200	60

Exercise 15:

a.   The warehouse estimates that it costs them $.25 per day for every printer held in inventory and it costs $300 for every order placed to the factory (regardless of the order size). The warehouse estimates that demand should remain about the same for the next 200 days (time units in SimQuick should represent days). For each scenario, run 100 simulations and report the overall mean service level and the estimated total cost. Which scenario would you recommend?

<u>Hint</u>: For the Exit in the model, you must enter statistical distributions for both "Time between departures" and "Num. objects per departure."

b.   The warehouse is considering using a different company to transport printers from the factory. The delivery time for this company can be estimated by a normal distribution with a mean of 4 days and a standard deviation of 1 day; however, the fixed cost per order would increase to $500. The warehouse believes this will allow them to significantly lower their reorder point, but will probably require them to increase their order size. For each scenario (row) in the following table, run 100 simulations and report the overall mean service level and the estimated total cost. Would you recommend switching delivery companies and, if so, which scenario would you recommend?

Order Size	Reorder Point
80	20
120	20
160	20
200	20
240	20

If you like, see Appendix 3 for how to use the feature Scenarios to run these model variations more efficiently.

Example 16: Two stores and a warehouse

This example builds on the electronics superstore and warehouse examples, by considering them simultaneously in a multi-level supply chain. Thus, the store management now has control of two levels of the supply chain. The key question is still: How much and when to order? However, management now must consider inventory that occurs in several places of the process, including the delivery trucks!

Consider a company that manages two electronics stores that sell the same popular handheld computer. Orders are placed to a regional warehouse, also owned by this company. The regional warehouse places orders to the manufacturer (which is not owned by the company). The amount of time to receive an order at either store can be approximated by a normal distribution with a mean of 1 day and a standard deviation of .1 days. The amount of time to receive an order at the warehouse can be approximated by a normal distribution, with a mean of 4 days and a standard deviation of .2 days. The mean demand for this computer at each store is five computers per day (both stores are open 10 hours per day, 7 days per week). The demand is expected to remain the same at both stores for the next 60 days.

Management wants to use a reorder point scheme at the stores and the warehouse. Their goal is to achieve at least a 95% service level at each store at minimum cost. The ordering costs are $75 every time a store places an order to the warehouse and $150 every time the warehouse places an order to the factory. It also costs $.50 per day for every computer in inventory at a store, and $.10

per day for every computer in inventory at the warehouse. We assume it also costs \$.10 per day for every computer in transit from the warehouse to a store.

Modeling the process with SimQuick

A process flow map is provided below.

Process Flow Map for Two Stores and a Warehouse

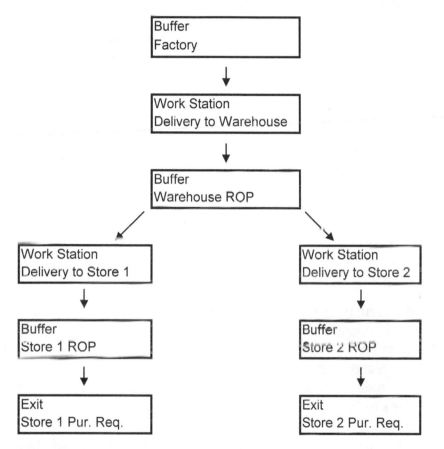

Let time units in SimQuick represent hours. Thus, the delivery time to the stores from the warehouse is modeled by Nor(10,1) and the delivery time to the warehouse from the factory is modeled by Nor(40,2).

Finally, let's consider how to calculate the cost of inventory in transit from the warehouse to the store. To begin, we calculate the mean inventory in transit to Store 1 (this is done similarly for Store 2):

$$\begin{pmatrix} \text{Mean in - transit} \\ \text{inventory to Store 1} \end{pmatrix} = \begin{pmatrix} \text{Overall mean of} \\ \text{"fraction of time working"} \\ \text{at Delivery to Store 1} \end{pmatrix} * (\text{Order size to Store 1})$$

We now get the following approximation:

The total cost of in-transit inventory (during the simulation) =

$$\left[\left(\begin{array}{c}\text{Mean in - transit}\\\text{inventory to Store 1}\end{array}\right)+\left(\begin{array}{c}\text{Mean in - transit}\\\text{inventory to Store 2}\end{array}\right)\right]*\left(\$.50\text{ per computer per day}\right)*\left(60\text{ days}\right)$$

Note that 60 days is the number of simulated days.

Exercise 16: Build the SimQuick model in Example 16. For each scenario (row) in the following table, run 100 simulations and report the mean of the overall mean service levels for the two stores and the estimated total cost. Which scenario should management adopt? (If you like, see Appendix 3 for how to use the feature Scenarios to run these model variations more efficiently.)

Warehouse ord. size	Warehouse ROP	Store ord. size	Store ROP
100	50	40	10
100	50	45	10
100	50	50	10
200	50	40	10
200	50	45	10
200	50	50	10

Note: Although it may not seem obvious at first, this example is a special case of the *just-in-time* (JIT) system typically used in manufacturing to control the flow of inventory in a factory or supply chain. In such systems customer demand depletes the inventory of an end product. When the inventory is depleted by a certain amount, a signal is sent to a supplying work station (or company) to replenish this amount of inventory. When the work station is free and its raw material is available, it starts to fill the replenishment request. When the raw material for this work station is depleted by a certain amount, a signal is sent to its supplying work station (or company); and so on. This is called a "pull" system because movements throughout the process are initiated by the removal of inventory at end of the process. In a more general JIT system, multiple replenishment orders can be placed as customer demand further reduces the inventory of end products. The note at the end of Exercise 19 in Chapter 4 contains an additional discussion of this strategy.

Section 3: More complex inventory models

This section contains models of two inventory policies that present some new challenges for modeling with SimQuick. One important modeling trick sets these models apart from those in the previous section: the use of Entrances to capture demand for the products instead of Exits. This trick allows orders to be backlogged. This trick also allows orders to the supplier to be triggered in more ways. In the first model, the base stock policy, orders are triggered immediately by sales; orders tend to be small and multiple orders can be outstanding. In the second model, a general periodic review policy, orders are triggered at fixed times and the amount ordered depends on the inventory level.

Example 17: An appliance store

An appliance store sells a popular refrigerator. This item is expensive and large, so the store keeps a limited number in inventory. When a customer wants to buy a refrigerator either the store has one in inventory, in which case one is immediately delivered to the customer, or it does not. In the latter case, the store has found that its customers are willing to make the purchase and wait a reasonable amount of time until a refrigerator arrives from the supplier. (A delayed customer order is called a *backlog*.) The store controls its inventory as follows: Whenever a refrigerator is delivered to a customer, the store orders a replacement from its supplier (hence replacement orders are triggered by customer deliveries and not new backlogs). As a result, there is a maximum number of refrigerators that the store can have in inventory; this number is called the *base stock level* and this simple inventory policy is called a *base stock policy*. The store sells, on average, one refrigerator per day (according to an exponential distribution). The amount of time for the store to receive an order from its supplier varies a bit: 25% of the time it takes two days, 50% of the time it takes three days, and 25% of the time it takes four days. The store is open 8 hours a day, 7 days a week.

Management wants to know the relationship between the base stock level and the average customer wait for delivery (a key service measure). In particular, they want to determine the base stock level so that customers don't have to wait more than a day, on average, to get their orders filled and, subject to this, they want to minimize their inventory costs: the sum of holding cost plus ordering cost.

The process flow map and some of the SimQuick tables for this model are shown below. Time units represent hours.

Process Flow Map for a Base Stock Policy

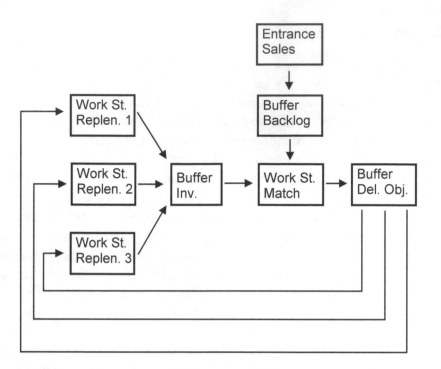

Entrance:

1	
Name →	Sales
Time between arrivals →	Exp(8)
Num. objects per arrival →	1
Output destination(s) ↓	
Backlog	

Buffers:

1			2	
Name →	Backlog		**Name →**	Inv.
Capacity →	Unlimited		Capacity →	Unlimited
Initial # objects →	0		Initial # objects →	3
Output destination(s) ↓	Output group size ↓		Output destination(s) ↓	Output group size ↓
Match	1		Match	1

3	
Name →	Del. Obj.
Capacity →›	Unlimited
Initial # objects →	0
Output destination(s) ↓	Output group size ↓
Replen. 1	1
Replen. 2	1
Replen. 3	1

Work Stations:

1			
Name →	Match		
Working time →	0		
Output destination(s) ↓	# of output objects ↓	Resource name(s) ↓	Resource # units needed ↓
Del. Obj.	1		

2			
Name →	Replen. 1		
Working time →	Dis(1)		
Output destination(s) ↓	# of output objects ↓	Resource name(s) ↓	Resource # units needed ↓
Inv.	1		

Discrete Distribution:

1	
Values ↓	Percents ↓
16	25
24	50
32	25

The refrigerators in inventory at the store arc represented by the objects in the Buffer called Inv. In this model there are 3 objects initially in inventory, which is the base stock level. Each sale of a refrigerator is modeled by an arrival of an object at the Entrance called Sales. Such objects immediately enter the large capacity Buffer called Backlog. The Work Station called Match has the job of matching sales with items in inventory. For Match to work, it must have one of each of its two inputs (in general, a Work Station must have available one of each of its inputs in order to start working). Hence, if there exists an object in Inv. (i.e., a refrigerator in inventory at the store) and if there exists an object in Backlog (i.e., a refrigerator has been sold), then one of each of these objects is taken by Match and a single object (representing a delivered refrigerator) is output to Del. Obj. (i.e., delivered objects). Notice that Match has working time equal to 0, hence this operation takes no time in the model. Also notice that if an object enters Backlog and there is no object in Inv., then this object will remain in Backlog until an object appears in Inv.

Hence, for our example, the mean cycle time of an object in Backlog is a measure of how long customers must wait for a refrigerator once it has been purchased.

Observe that an object enters Del. Obj. precisely when a replenishment order should be placed. The model captures this by immediately sending such an object to one of the three Work Stations, called Replen. 1–3 (where Replen. stands for replenishment order). The Replen. Work Stations model the actual deliveries of individual refrigerators; the working time for each is given by the Discrete Distribution table 1. (These tables can be found in SimQuick by clicking on "Other Features" followed by "Discrete Distributions"; the numbers in the Values column are the possible working times for the Work Station and they are randomly chosen according to the probabilities in the Percents column; the number in parentheses of Dis() is always the corresponding table number. See Example 11 for an introduction to Discrete Distributions.) In other words, as soon as an object is removed from Inv., one of the Replen. Work Stations starts working, thus modeling a replenishment order being sent from the supplier. Notice that since there are three replenishment Work Stations and the base stock level is 3, we can always immediately place a replenishment order.

The above model can easily be modified to capture policy variations such as the following: only place replenishment orders after two refrigerators have been delivered. Thus the supplier sends two refrigerators at a time. The tables are modified by setting each of the output group sizes of Del. Obj. to be 2 and setting the Number of output objects of each Replen. Work Station to be 2. This variation will likely result in fewer shipments but longer customer waiting. Of course, 2 can be replaced here with any larger number.

It's also important to note that, in general, the number of Work Stations called Replen. must be greater than or equal to the base stock level, since this is the maximum number of simultaneous replenishment orders.

Below is some of the output from 100 simulations of the model. Demand is expected to remain stable for this product for the next two months (60 days), so these simulations were run for 480 time units (= (60 days)*(8 hours per day)).

Simulation Results

Return to Control Panel

Element types	Element names	Statistics	Overall means	Simulation Numbers 1	2
Work Station(s)	Match	Final status	NA	Not Working	Not Working
		Final inventory (int. buff.)	0.00	0	0
		Mean inventory (int. buff.)	0.00	0.00	0.00
		Mean cycle time (int. buff.)	0.00	0.00	0.00
		Work cycles started	54.84	49	54
		Fraction time working	0.00	0.00	0.00
		Fraction time blocked	0.00	0.00	0.00
	Replen. 1	Final status	NA	Working	Working
		Final inventory (int. buff.)	0.00	0	0
		Mean inventory (int. buff.)	0.00	0.00	0.00
		Mean cycle time (int. buff.)	0.00	0.00	0.00
		Work cycles started	18.97	19	18
		Fraction time working	0.93	0.90	0.92
		Fraction time blocked	0.00	0.00	0.00
	Replen. 2	Final status	NA	Working	Working
		Final inventory (int. buff.)	0.00	0	0
		Mean inventory (int. buff.)	0.00	0.00	0.00
		Mean cycle time (int. buff.)	0.00	0.00	0.00
		Work cycles started	18.33	16	19
		Fraction time working	0.89	0.79	0.89
		Fraction time blocked	0.00	0.00	0.00
	Replen. 3	Final status	NA	Working	Working
		Final inventory (int. buff.)	0.00	0	0
		Mean inventory (int. buff.)	0.00	0.00	0.00
		Mean cycle time (int. buff.)	0.00	0.00	0.00
		Work cycles started	17.54	14	17
		Fraction time working	0.95	0.64	0.78
		Fraction time blocked	0.00	0.00	0.00
Buffer(s)	Backlog	Objects leaving	54.84	40	54
		Final inventory	5.88	1	2
		Minimum inventory	0.00	0	0
		Maximum inventory	9.53	3	8
		Mean inventory	3.51	0.41	2.26
		Mean cycle time	30.04	4.03	20.12
	Inv.	Objects leaving	54.84	49	54
		Final inventory	0.16	0	0
		Minimum inventory	0.00	0	0
		Maximum inventory	3.00	3	3
		Mean inventory	0.33	0.67	0.41
		Mean cycle time	3.01	6.56	3.68

The amount of time a customer waits to receive his order is approximated by the overall mean cycle time of Backlog, which is 30.04 time units (or hours). This clearly exceeds management's goal of having customers wait a day (or 8 time units), on average. Hence it appears that the base stock level must be increased.

A final consideration is the cost. The cost of each shipment from the supplier is roughly $150. The overall mean number of orders placed in our simulations is the sum of the overall mean number of Work cycles started at the three Replen. Work Stations, which is 54.84 (= 18.97 + 18.33 + 17.54). Hence, we may estimate the store's overall mean ordering cost during the simulations to be ($150 per order)*(54.84 orders) = $8226.00. The cost of holding a refrigerator in inventory is roughly $1.00 per day. The overall mean number of refrigerators in inventory in our simulations is the overall mean inventory of Inv., which is .33. Hence, we may estimate the store's holding cost during the simulations to be (60 days)*($1.00 per day per refrigerator)*(.33 refrigerators) = $19.80. So the total cost is $8226.00 + $19.80 = $8245.80. Clearly the cost is dominated, in this example, by the ordering cost.

Management has decided to consider a number of different scenarios in looking for a solution to their inventory problem. These scenarios are summarized by the rows in the following table.

Order size	Base stock level
1	4
1	5
1	6
2	3
2	4
2	5
2	6

Exercise 17: For each scenario in the above table, run 100 simulations and report estimates for the customer waiting time, mean number of backlogged orders, mean inventory of refrigerators in the store, ordering cost, holding cost, and total cost. Report the lowest cost scenario that achieves management's goal for customer waiting time.

Hint: Build your model just once with six Replen. Work Stations; then you only need to vary the output group size from Del. Obj. and the # of output objects from the Replen. Work Stations for each scenario. Also, see Appendix 3 for how to use the feature Scenarios to run these model variations even more efficiently.

Example 18: A department store

A department store sells a line of blue jeans. Recent sales records show that, on average, one pairs of jeans is sold every hour (according to an exponential distribution). Every Monday, if necessary, the store places a replenishment order to its supplier. Orders take two, three, or four days (with probabilities 20%, 60%, and 20%, respectively) to arrive. When it's time to order, the order size is determined from three factors: the current inventory level; the allowable order sizes of 20, 40, or 60 pairs of jeans (jeans must be ordered in multiples of 20); and a target value of 80. The order size is calculated as follows: take the target value minus the current inventory level and round down to the nearest allowable order size (if there is one). For example, suppose the inventory level is 38 pairs of jeans. Then the store will order 40 pairs, since $80 - 38 = 42$, which rounds down to the allowable order size of 40. Notice that an order will only be placed if the current inventory is 60 or fewer pairs of jeans; 60 is equal to the target value minus the smallest allowable order size.

Because orders are only placed at regularly spaced times, this inventory strategy is called a *periodic review policy*. In this example, the allowable order sizes are limited to multiples of 20 by the supplier. In general, management can vary the numbers on the list of allowable order sizes (and the length of the list) as well as the target value (as long as the target value is greater than or equal to each of the allowable order sizes). Management's goal is to find the best combination of these numbers that delivers the desired service level to the customers and, subject to this, minimizes the holding and ordering costs.

The process flow map and some of the SimQuick tables for this model are shown below. Time units represent hours and the store is open 10 hours a day, 7 days a week.

Process Flow Map for a Periodic Review Policy

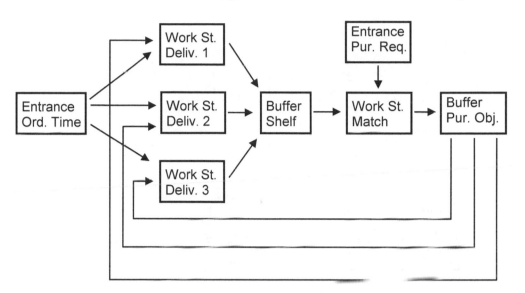

Entrances:

1	
Name →	Pur. Req.
Time between arrivals →	Exp(1)
Num. objects per arrival →	1
Output destination(s) ↓	
Match	

2	
Name →	Ord. Time
Time between arrivals →	70
Num. objects per arrival →	1
Output destination(s) ↓	
Deliv. 1	
Deliv. 2	
Deliv. 3	

Work Stations:

1			
Name →	Match		
Working time →	0		
Output destination(s) ↓	# of output objects ↓	Resource name(s) ↓	Resource # units needed ↓
Pur. Obj.	1		

2			
Name →	Deliv. 1		
Working time →	Dis(1)		
Output destination(s) ↓	# of output objects ↓	Resource name(s) ↓	Resource # units needed ↓
Shelf	60		

73

	3	
Name →	Deliv. 2	
Working time →	Dis(1)	

Output destination(s) ↓	# of output objects ↓	Resource name(s) ↓	Resource # units needed ↓
Shelf	40		

Buffers:

	4	
Name →	Deliv. 3	
Working time →	Dis(1)	

Output destination(s) ↓	# of output objects ↓	Resource name(s) ↓	Resource # units needed ↓
Shelf	20		

1			2	
Name →	Shelf		**Name →**	Pur. Obj.
Capacity →	Unlimited		Capacity →	Unlimited
Initial # objects →	80		Initial # objects →	0

Output destination(s) ↓	Output group size ↓		Output destination(s) ↓	Output group size ↓
Match	1		Deliv. 1	60
			Deliv. 2	40
			Deliv. 3	20

Discrete Distribution:

1	
Values ↓	Percents ↓
20	20
30	60
40	20

The jeans in inventory at the store are represented by the objects in the Buffer called Shelf. In this model there are 80 objects initially in inventory, which is the target value. Each request for a pair of jeans is modeled by an arrival of an object at the Entrance called Pur. Req. (i.e., purchase requests). The job of the Work Station called Match is to match purchase requests with items in inventory. For Match to work it must have one of each of its two inputs (recall that, in general, a Work Station must have one of each of its inputs in order to begin working). So, if there is an object in Shelf when an object arrives at Pur. Req., then Match will take these two objects and output an object to Pur. Obj. (i.e., the purchased objects). Since Match has working time equal to 0, this operation takes no time in the model. If there is no object in Shelf when an object arrives at Pur. Req., then Match does nothing and the object at Pur. Req. leaves the model. Hence the service level of Pur. Req. will tell us the fraction of purchase requests that are satisfied.

Once every 70 time units (i.e., once a week) a single object arrives at the Entrance called Ord. Time (i.e., order time). These arrivals correspond to the times that orders may be placed. Let us suppose such an object has just arrived during a simulation. Such an object can provide one of the two inputs that each of the three Work Stations called Deliv. (i.e., delivery) needs to work. The other object needed must come from Pur. Obj. Observe that each object output by Pur. Obj. is a batch whose size corresponds to one of the numbers on the list of allowable order sizes. In our example, suppose there are 43 objects in Pur. Obj.; note that 43 is the target value minus the current inventory level. Then, according to our inventory policy, we should place an order for 40 objects. Pur. Obj. can output either one object to Deliv. 2, corresponding to a batch of 40 objects, or one object to Deliv. 3, corresponding to a batch of 20 objects. Hence both Work Stations Deliv. 2 and Deliv. 3 have both their inputs and are ready to work. When two Work Stations in SimQuick are competing for limited inputs, the Work Station with higher *priority* gets the inputs. The priority of a Work Station is determined by the number of the table into which it has been entered (the lower the number, the higher the priority). Thus, in our example, Deliv. 2 will take in its two inputs and begin working while Deliv. 3 will remain idle. Hence the number of objects in Pur. Obj. decreases by 40. The actual deliveries of the jeans are then modeled by the Deliv. Work Stations, which output the appropriate quantities to Shelf. Because the delivery times are less than the time between orders, no more than one order is placed at a time, hence this model implements the periodic review policy used by this store.

Below are the results from 100 simulations of the present inventory policy (only the details from the first two simulations are displayed). The demand pattern is expected to remain stable for the next 90 days, hence each simulation is run for 900 time units (= (90 days)*(10 hours per day))

Simulation Results

Return to Control Panel

Element types	Element names	Statistics	Overall means	Simulation Numbers 1	2
Entrance(s)	Pur. Req.	Objects entering process	693.82	716	663
		Objects unable to enter	197.89	173	160
		Service level	0.78	0.81	0.81
	Ord. Time	Objects entering process	12.00	12	12
		Objects unable to enter	1.00	1	1
		Service level	0.92	0.92	0.92
Work Station(s)	Match	Final status	NA	Not Working	Not Working
		Final inventory (int. buff.)	0.00	0	0
		Mean inventory (int. buff.)	0.00	0.00	0.00
		Mean cycle time (int. buff.)	0.00	0.00	0.00
		Work cycles started	693.82	716	663
		Fraction time working	0.00	0.00	0.00
		Fraction time blocked	0.00	0.00	0.00
	Deliv. 1	Final status	NA	Not Working	Not Working
		Final inventory (int. buff.)	0.00	0	0
		Mean inventory (int. buff.)	0.00	0.00	0.00
		Mean cycle time (int. buff.)	0.00	0.00	0.00
		Work cycles started	7.96	9	7
		Fraction time working	0.27	0.29	0.27
		Fraction time blocked	0.00	0.00	0.00
	Deliv. 2	Final status	NA	Not Working	Not Working
		Final inventory (int. buff.)	0.00	0	0
		Mean inventory (int. buff.)	0.00	0.00	0.00
		Mean cycle time (int. buff.)	0.00	0.00	0.00
		Work cycles started	3.99	3	5
		Fraction time working	0.13	0.08	0.17
		Fraction time blocked	0.00	0.00	0.00
	Deliv. 3	Final status	NA	Not Working	Not Working
		Final inventory (int. buff.)	0.00	0	0
		Mean inventory (int. buff.)	0.00	0.00	0.00
		Mean cycle time (int. buff.)	Infinite	Infinite	Infinite
		Work cycles started	0.05	0	0
		Fraction time working	0.00	0.00	0.00
		Fraction time blocked	0.00	0.00	0.00
Buffer(s)	Shelf	Objects leaving	693.82	716	663
		Final inventory	24.38	24	37
		Minimum inventory	0.00	0	0
		Maximum inventory	80.00	80	80
		Mean inventory	23.82	24.55	22.31
		Mean cycle time	30.91	30.86	30.29
	Pur. Obj.	Objects leaving	638.20	660	620
		Final inventory	55.62	56	43
		Minimum inventory	0.00	0	0
		Maximum inventory	79.71	80	80
		Mean inventory	34.86	35.01	35.02
		Mean cycle time	49.22	47.74	50.84

Observe that the overall mean service level is .78, which is below management's goal of satisfying 90% of the customer demand. The service level can be increased by increasing the largest allowable order size; hence the target value may also have to be increased.

Finally, let's consider how to calculate the costs of this policy. The store pays $50 for every order it places. The overall mean number of orders placed in our simulations is the overall mean number of objects entering the process at Ord. time. In this case, that number is 12. (The one object that was unable to enter Ord. Time in each simulation was the initial one that appeared at the beginning of each simulation; hence in each simulation we placed subsequent orders at every opportunity.) We may estimate the store's ordering cost during the simulations to be ($50 per order)*(12 orders) = $600. The store also pays $.05 per day for every pair of jeans on the shelf.

The overall mean number of jeans on the shelf is the overall mean inventory of Shelf. Hence we may estimate the store's holding cost during the simulations to be (90 days)*($.05 per day)*(23.82) = $107.19. So the total inventory cost is $600 + $107.19 = $707.19.

Management is considering the following scenarios (each row) of allowable order sizes and target values:

Allowable order sizes			Target values
20	60	100	100
20	60	100	120
40	60	100	100
40	60	100	120
40	60	120	120

Exercise 18:

a. For each scenario in the above table, run 100 simulations and report the overall mean service level and the estimated cost. Report the lowest cost scenario that achieves a service level of at least .9.

b. Can you find a better scenario? You may also try varying the time between orders from every 7 days to every 10 days.

   If you like, see Appendix 3 for how to use the feature Scenarios to run these model variations more efficiently.

Chapter 4: Manufacturing

Learning objectives:

- To model, simulate, and analyze the following types of processes: linear flow, cellular, assembly/disassembly, batch, and job shop.
- To model and analyze the following features of a process: quality testing and machine breakdowns.
- To understand the following performance measures: throughput, cycle time, mean inventory level, service level, utilization, flow time, and tardiness.
- To understand the following concepts: bottleneck, setup, and batch size.
- To understand the following priority rules: shortest processing time and nearest due date.
- To understand the trade-offs between working time variability, inventory level, and throughput; number of workers and throughput; and batch size and service level.
- To understand the SimQuick features of Resources and Priorities.

Overview

In this chapter, we discuss a variety of process types typically associated with manufacturing. We consider processes where products are made in a line (including cellular manufacturing), where products are split apart and reassembled, where products are made in batches, and where many different products may go through the same machine (a job shop). We also consider processes where something can go wrong in either the form of a quality problem with a product or a reliability problem with a machine.

In most cases, the performance measure that most interests us is the *capacity* of the process; that is, we want to study the maximum amount that can be produced during some time period. This is also sometimes called the *throughput* of the process. Thus, we do not explicitly incorporate customer demand into most of these models (although it can easily be added). In the batch process example, customer demand is included in the model and service level becomes a key performance measure. In the job shop example, we are interested in two different performance measures: the average production time (i.e., the mean cycle time or mean *flow time* or mean *lead time*) and the on-time performance (in particular, the mean *tardiness*). These measures will be defined in the examples.

In the linear flow process, we examine the trade-offs between working time variability, inventory level, and throughput. We also look at how, over the long run, inventory tends to pile up, filling the available space. In the cellular manufacturing process, we examine the trade-off between the number of workers and the throughput. In the assembly/disassembly process, we examine how to identify a bottleneck (by considering *utilization*) and the effect on throughput of reducing the bottleneck. In the batch process example, the concepts of *batch size* and *setups* are introduced and the trade-off between batch size and service level is examined.

In general, the processes considered in this chapter are parts of larger processes. Thus, the processes in this chapter may be thought of as building blocks for more complex processes. For example, the processes in this chapter may be combined with the inventory in supply chain processes from the previous chapter.

The cellular manufacturing, job shop, quality, and reliability processes make use of the advanced SimQuick features called Resources and Priorities (which are first introduced in Example 12).

Section 1: Linear flow processes

By a linear flow process, we mean a process that can be modeled as a series of Buffers and Work Stations, possibly with an Entrance at one end and an Exit at the other end. Hence, objects are passed from one element to the next as capacity, demand, and supply dictate. Processes of this type are common in factories. Examples include the manufacturing of home appliances, computer equipment, and automobiles.

The first example we consider is a generic small model. What makes this model interesting is the variation in the working times at the Work Stations. As the exercise demonstrates, this variation plays an important role in the performance of the process.

In the second example, we consider a special type of linear flow process called a *cell*. In this type of process, the work stations are very close together. This has two effects: The amount of inventory is typically low and workers can operate more than one machine. In this example, we consider the performance of the process with various numbers of workers.

Example 19: A generic linear flow process

In this example, we consider a simple process described by the following process flow map:

Process Flow Map for a Linear Flow Process

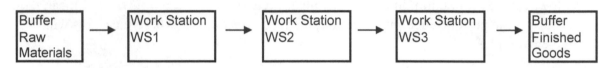

We let time units denote minutes. The working time at each Work Station is uncertain, but can be approximated the same way: by a uniform distribution with a minimum of 5 minutes and maximum of 15 minutes (i.e., enter Uni(5,15) for the working times). Hence, the line is *balanced* in the sense that the mean working time (10 minutes) at each Work Station is the same (however, there is a lot of variance in the working times). We run the model for a simulated 24-hour time period, that is, 1440 time units. For the capacity and initial inventory of Raw Materials, enter 200 (this will prevent us from running out). Enter Unlimited for the capacity of Finished Goods (its initial inventory should be 0).

We could easily make the model more realistic by incorporating an Entrance for the raw materials and an Exit for the finished goods (which would allow us to model arrivals and departures from the process due to, say, trucking schedules; in fact, this is done in Appendix 3). By keeping things simple for now, we can examine, in the exercise, some key relationships involving the following: inventory (between the Work Stations), variability (in working times), throughput (the number of finished goods produced per day), cycle time, and length of the simulation.

Due to the variability in working times, the following situation is likely to occur when you run this model in SimQuick: WS2 finishes working on an object, while WS3 is still working on another object. When this happens, WS2 puts its finished object into its internal buffer, which can hold only one object in this model. Until this object has been passed to WS3, WS2 cannot start working on a new object. WS2 is said to be *blocked* while it is waiting for WS3 to finish. You can learn what fraction of the entire simulation WS2 is blocked by looking on the Results sheet under "Fraction time blocked" for WS2.

Note: A conveyor in a factory can also be modeled by a sequence of Work Stations. The number of Work Stations should be the maximum number of objects that can be on the conveyor at one time. The working time at each Work Station should be a constant; this constant should simply be the amount of time it takes an object to traverse the conveyor divided by the number of Work Stations in the model.

Exercise 19: For each of the situations a through e below, perform 100 simulations and report the overall mean throughput (i.e., the overall mean <u>final</u> inventory of Buffer: Finished Goods). Also report the overall mean cycle time through the process from the time it enters WS1 to the time it leaves WS3. This is computed by adding the overall mean cycle times through the internal buffers, the Buffers added between Work Stations, and the mean working times at the Work Stations.

a.   Consider the SimQuick model described above. Note that the working time for each Work Station is Uni(5,15).

b.   Consider the original model, changing the working time at each Work Station to Uni(9,11). Note that the new working times have the same mean but a smaller variance.

c.   Consider the original model, using the reduced variance distribution from part b on WS2 only.

d.   For the original model, add a Buffer between WS1 and WS2 and another Buffer between WS2 and WS3 (with no initial inventory). Consider the five scenarios where the capacity of both Buffers is set to 1, then 3, then 5, then 7, and then 9.

e.   Consider the model in d (with the capacities of the added Buffers at 9), using the reduced variance distributions from b.

f.   Summarize your results from parts a through e. In particular, discuss the relationship between inventory, working time variability, throughput, and cycle time.

g.   Consider the model in d, except set the capacities of the added Buffers and Finished Goods to be Unlimited. Run the model for 2000, then 5000, then 10000 time units. Make sure you increase the initial inventory in Raw Materials so you don't run out during the simulations. In each case, report the overall mean inventory and the overall mean maximum inventory in both of the added Buffers. What does this imply about inventory levels in a factory where Buffer sizes are large and production runs are long?

Note: In parts a–f, we have limited the amount of inventory allowed between Work Stations (for example, the inventory capacity between WS1 and WS2 is the one object capacity of the internal buffer of WS1 plus the capacity of the added Buffer, if there is one). These limits control the way objects flow through the process and have an interesting interpretation. Let us interpret every object that enters WS3 as a purchase of an object by a customer (hence the time between purchases is random). Assume that during a simulation there has not been a purchase for some time and that the buffer spaces between WS1 and WS2 and between WS2 and WS3 are full. It follows that WS1 and WS2 are blocked and no objects can move in the model. Objects can only move again when a purchase is made. When this occurs, the number of objects between WS2 and WS3 decreases by one. This serves as a signal to WS2 to begin working and it removes an object from between WS1 and WS2. This then serves as a signal to WS1 to begin working. In a real process, an inventory limit between work stations is sometimes enforced with *kanbans* (a simple system involving the use of cards). This is a key component in many JIT processes (which are also sometimes called "pull" systems). Observe that a model almost equivalent to the one just discussed can be obtained by replacing WS3 and Finished Goods with an Exit (see Example 13 for an introduction to Exits).

Example 20: A Manufacturing Cell

For this example, we consider a linear flow process where the work stations are close together and hence there is little room for inventory between stations. When a process of this type consists of machines arranged in a "U-shape" in a factory, it is often called a *cell*. The reason for a U-shaped configuration is to make it more convenient for each worker to operate two or more machines. In this example, we are interested in the effect on throughput of using 6 vs. 3 vs. 2 workers in this cell. We assume here that when a machine is running, it must be attended by a worker (hence, a worker cannot start a machine working on a part and then go do something else while it's working). We consider a process with the following flow map.

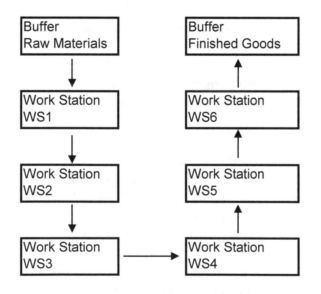

Process Flow Map for Cellular Manufacturing

As in Example 19, time units represent minutes and we assume that the working time at each Work Station can be approximated by a uniform distribution with minimum value 5 and maximum value 15. If we enter this model as usual into SimQuick, then we are modeling the situation where each machine has its own dedicated worker.

Next, we consider the case of running the cell with three workers. (The case with two workers is left to the reader.) Let's say that Worker 1 is assigned to WS1 and WS2, Worker 2 is assigned to WS3 and WS4, and Worker 3 is assigned to WS5 and WS6. These workers are modeled in SimQuick as Resources. When using Resources in SimQuick, we must inform SimQuick how many of each we have available. To do this, click the "Other Features" button followed by the "Resources" button. Fill in the table as follows:

Name ↓	Number available ↓
Worker 1	1
Worker 2	1
Worker 3	1

In this case, we have only one of each worker available. However, a Resource could represent a group of people (e.g., maintenance workers) or a set of identical tools, in which case there could be more than one available.

From the Control Panel, click on "Work Stations." Fill in tables 1 and 2 as follows. (Note how we are assigning the Resource Worker 1 to WS1 and WS2.)

1

	Name →	WS1	
	Working time →	Uni(5,15)	
Output destination(s) ↓	# of output objects ↓	Resource name(s) ↓	Resource # units needed ↓
WS2	1	Worker 1	1

2

	Name →	WS2	
	Working time →	Uni(5,15)	
Output destination(s) ↓	# of output objects ↓	Resource name(s) ↓	Resource # units needed ↓
WS3	1	Worker 1	1

Similarly, fill in the tables for WS3 and WS4 with Worker 2 and fill in the tables for WS5 and WS6 with Worker 3.

Here is what happens when SimQuick runs. If a Work Station is not working, if it contains no finished object in its internal buffer, if there is an input object available, and if the Resource it requires is available, then it takes the input object and the Resource and begins working. The Resource then becomes unavailable to other Work Stations. When a Work Station finishes working on an object, it makes the Resource available to other Work Stations. In this model, this means that each worker will alternate between his or her two machines, working on one object each time.

Observe that when a model with Resources is run, the Results sheet reports the "Mean number in use" for each Resource.

Exercise 20: Run 100 simulations for each of the situations described above: with six, three, and two workers. (For the two-worker case, assign one worker to WS1, WS2, and WS3 and assign the other worker to the other Work Stations.) Run each simulation for 1440 time units (i.e., 24 simulated hours). Make sure you set the capacity and initial number of objects for Raw Materials and the capacity of Finished Goods to be sufficiently large (200 will do the job). Report the overall mean throughput for each case (i.e., the overall mean <u>final</u> inventory in Finished Goods). Also report the overall mean throughput divided by the number of workers for each situation. Which situation has the best throughput per worker?

Section 2: Assembly/disassembly processes

In this section, we consider two common activities in a process: taking several different parts and combining them into one part (assembly), and taking one part and breaking it into several different parts (disassembly). This is easy to model with SimQuick.

Example 21: Box manufacturing

Here we describe a (simplified) process for making wooden jewelry boxes. Each box is made from the following parts: two identical square pieces (the top and bottom), four identical rectangular pieces (the sides), and a hinge. At the beginning of the process is a pile of sheets of wood. One sheet at a time is taken to a machine, called Cutter. From each sheet, this machine cuts out four square pieces and eight rectangular pieces. (Note that the Cutter produces enough for two boxes due to the size of the sheets.) The four square pieces are then sent to a Buffer, followed by a machine, called TB Finishing, for making them into tops and bottoms, followed by another Buffer. The eight rectangular pieces are also sent to a Buffer, followed by a machine, called S Finishing, for making them into sides, followed by another Buffer. A Work Station, called Box Assembly, then takes a top, a bottom, and four sides and constructs boxes, one at a time. Further details are provided below.

Management believes the machine S Finishing is a *bottleneck*. This means they believe that, if this machine were replaced with a faster machine, the number of boxes produced each day (i.e., the *throughput*) would increase. In particular, management wants to know how much the throughput would increase if the machine were replaced with a new machine whose working time can be approximated by a normal distribution with a mean of 2.5 minutes and a standard deviation of .5 minutes.

Modeling the process with SimQuick

The following process flow map describes the present process:

Process Flow Map for Box Manufacturing

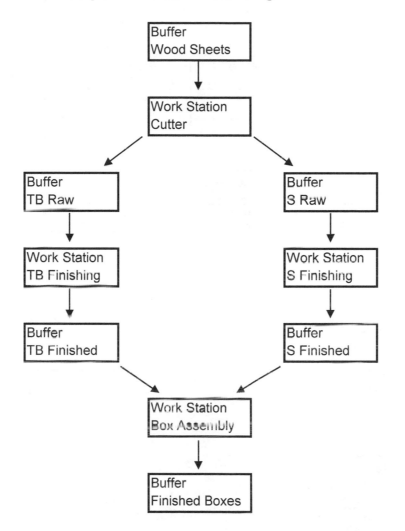

Next, we present the SimQuick model. Time units represent minutes. Note that for the Work Stations we have added statistical distributions that approximate the "real" working times and for the Buffers we have added capacities and estimates of typical initial inventory levels.

Work Stations:

	1		
Name →	Cutter		
Working time →	Nor(10,1)		
Output destination(s) ↓	# of output objects ↓	Resource name(s) ↓	Resource # units needed ↓
TB Raw	4		
S Raw	8		

2			
Name →		TB Finishing	
Working time →		Nor(5,1)	
Output destination(s) ↓	# of output objects ↓	Resource name(s) ↓	Resource # units needed ↓
TB Finished	1		

3			
Name →		S Finishing	
Working time →		Nor(4,1)	
Output destination(s) ↓	# of output objects ↓	Resource name(s) ↓	Resource # units needed ↓
S Finished	1		

4			
Name →		Box Assembly	
Working time →		Nor(10,2)	
Output destination(s) ↓	# of output objects ↓	Resource name(s) ↓	Resource # units needed ↓
Finished Boxes	1		

Buffers:

1	
Name →	Wood Sheets
Capacity →	100
Initial # objects →	100
Output destination(s) ↓	Output group size ↓
Cutter	1

2	
Name →	TB Raw
Capacity →	10
Initial # objects →	2
Output destination(s) ↓	Output group size ↓
TB Finishing	1

3	
Name →	S Raw
Capacity →	20
Initial # objects →	20
Output destination(s) ↓	Output group size ↓
S Finishing	1

4	
Name →	TB Finished
Capacity →	10
Initial # objects →	8
Output destination(s) ↓	Output group size ↓
Box Assembly	2

5	
Name →	S Finished
Capacity →	20
Initial # objects →	0
Output destination(s) ↓	Output group size ↓
Box Assembly	4

6	
Name →	Finished Boxes
Capacity →	500
Initial # objects →	0
Output destination(s) ↓	Output group size ↓

Let's consider the Work Station called Cutter. First, observe that it has one input, the Buffer called Wood Sheets. Hence, this Work Station takes one object at a time from Wood Sheets and works on it. However, this Work Station has two outputs: TB Raw and S Raw, with "# of output objects" of 4 and 8, respectively. Hence, after finishing a work cycle, this Work Station sends 4 objects to TB Raw and 8 objects to S Raw (i.e., it takes 1 object in and sends 12 objects out). The working time Nor(10,1) represents the amount of time to cut one wood sheet into 12 pieces. In general, a Work Station with two or more outputs can be said to be performing a *disassembly* (in addition to splitting materials into pieces, multiple outputs can be used, for example, to model the disassembly of a machine at a maintenance center).

These objects then work their way through the Work Stations called TB Finishing and S Finishing, one at a time. Next observe that the Buffers called TB Finished and S Finished have "Output group sizes" of 2 and 4, respectively. This means that objects leave these Buffers 2 and 4 at a time, respectively, and that these groups of 2 and 4 are each considered to be a single object.

Finally, let's consider the Work Station called Box Assembly. It has two inputs. When a Work Station has more than one input, it cannot start a work cycle until it has one of each type of input. In this case, this means that the Box Assembly cannot start working until there are at least 2 objects in TB Finished (which are considered as a single object for output to Box Assembly) and 4 objects in S Finished (which are considered as a single object for output to Box Assembly). When one of each input object is available, a Work Station takes them and starts working. Thus, multiple inputs into a Work Station can be used to model an *assembly* operation.

Note 1: A Work Station can have both multiple inputs and multiple outputs.

Note 2: Multiple inputs and outputs can also be used to model "signaling," where a Work Station sends a message to another Work Station to begin working (see Example 22).

Exercise 21: Perform 100 simulations with the SimQuick model of the existing process and report the throughput (i.e., the overall mean <u>final</u> inventory in Finished Boxes). Run each simulation for 480 simulated minutes. Also report the overall mean fraction time working (also called *utilization*) for each Work Station. Which Work Station is a *bottleneck* according to this statistic (i.e., has highest value)? Rerun the simulations with the new Work Station and report the same statistics. Is there a significant improvement in throughput? Is the work more evenly balanced between the Work Stations (i.e., the overall mean fraction time working)?

Section 3: Batch and job shop processes

In this section, we consider two important types of processes. Both are fairly complex in that they involve special rules that create new modeling challenges. Batch processes are used, for example, in the manufacturing of food, clothing, and pharmaceuticals. Batch processes typically have a machine that is used to manufacture several different products. It is time consuming and expensive to switch the machine from making one product to another; such a switch is called a *setup*. Thus, each product is made in fairly large batches. The result is that inventory can pile up. Hence, an important question: How large should these batches be so that demand is satisfied and inventory does not pile up too much? We consider this question in Example 22.

Job shop processes are used, for example, in the manufacturing of machine parts, in the maintenance of jet engines, and for the care of patients in a hospital. Job shops typically have a variety of work stations and can make a variety of different products. With so many different types of jobs moving through a job shop at a time, an important question becomes the following: In what order should jobs be processed at each machine? We consider this question in Example 23.

Example 22: Pharmaceutical manufacturing

A pharmaceutical company makes a number of products in pill form. Two such products, Aspirin A and Aspirin B, have a high and steady demand and a single machine has been dedicated to making them. This machine can only make one type of pill at a time and must be thoroughly cleaned (i.e., *setup*) when it switches from making one type of pill to another. Management must decide how much of each type of pill to make at a time to satisfy 90% of the demand for each product; in operations lingo, management must decide on the best *batch sizes*.

Let us simplify the process as follows. First, assume we have as much raw material (chemicals in powder form) as we need. (Once we design the rest of the process, we can arrange with our supplier to deliver the quantities we need, when we need them.) The raw materials can be grouped into batches of anywhere from 100 to 500 lbs (in increments of 100 lbs). Batches are sent to the machine that creates the pills (pills are created by applying enormous pressure to the chemicals placed into pill-shaped molds). Every time the machine finishes a batch, it must be washed out before a batch of the other product can be started. The setup times are normally distributed with a mean of 3 working hours and a standard deviation of .5 hours. Actual processing times for a batch are the same for each product and are provided in the following table.

	Batch Sizes (lbs.)				
	100	200	300	400	500
Processing Times (hr)	Nor(1,.5)	Nor(2,.6)	Nor(3,.7)	Nor(4,.8)	Nor(5,.9)

After processing, the pills go into a storage area with a very large capacity. Pills are removed from the storage area as demand dictates: The time between shipments for Aspirin A is exponentially distributed with a mean of 20 working hours and each shipment is 300 lbs (or as much as is available); the time between shipments for Aspirin B is exponentially distributed with a mean of 10 working hours and each shipment is 300 lbs (or as much as is available).

Management is considering the following scenarios, or combinations of batch sizes.

	Scenarios (batch sizes in lbs)					
	1	2	3	4	5	6
Aspirin A	100	100	200	300	300	400
Aspirin B	200	300	300	400	500	500

For example, under scenario 1, 100 lbs of Aspirin A followed by 200 lbs of Aspirin B are made on the machine, then the pattern is repeated. Management wants to know how much finished inventory and what service level would result from each scenario.

Modeling the process with SimQuick

A process flow map and SimQuick model follow. The SimQuick tables are filled out for scenario 6. Each object corresponds to 100 lbs of materials (either raw materials or finished pills). Time units correspond to hours.

Process Flow Map for a Batch Process

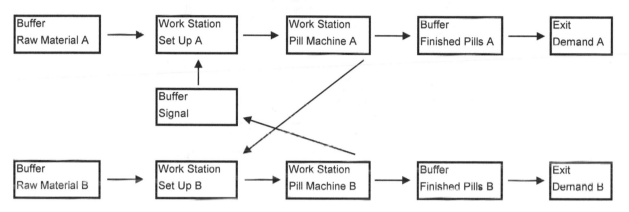

Buffers:

1	
Name →	Raw Material A
Capacity →	500
Initial # objects →	500
Output destination(s) ↓	Output group size ↓
Set Up A	4

2	
Name →	Finished Pills A
Capacity →	500
Initial # objects →	10
Output destination(s) ↓	Output group size ↓
Demand A	1

3	
Name →	Raw Material B
Capacity →	500
Initial # objects →	500
Output destination(s) ↓	Output group size ↓
Set Up B	5

4	
Name →	Finished Pills B
Capacity →	500
Initial # objects →	10
Output destination(s) ↓	Output group size ↓
Demand B	1

5	
Name →	Signal
Capacity →	1
Initial # objects →	1
Output destination(s) ↓	Output group size ↓
Set Up A	1

Work Stations:

1		
Name →	Set Up A	
Working time →	Nor(3,.5)	
Output destination(s) ↓	# of output objects ↓	Resource name(s) ↓	Resource # units needed ↓
Pill Machine A	1		

2		
Name →	Pill Machine A	
Working time →	Nor(4,.8)	
Output destination(s) ↓	# of output objects ↓	Resource name(s) ↓	Resource # units needed ↓
Finished Pills A	4		
Set Up B	1		

3		
Name →	Set Up B	
Working time →	Nor(3,.5)	
Output destination(s) ↓	# of output objects ↓	Resource name(s) ↓	Resource # units needed ↓
Pill Machine B	1		

4		
Name →	Pill Machine B	
Working time →	Nor(5,.9)	
Output destination(s) ↓	# of output objects ↓	Resource name(s) ↓	Resource # units needed ↓
Finished Pills B	5		
Signal	1		

Exits:

1		2	
Name →	Demand A	**Name** →	Demand B
Time between departures →	Exp(20)	Time between departures →	Exp(10)
Num. objects per departure →	3	Num. objects per departure →	3

Let's consider how this model works (using the numbers for scenario 6). The real pill machine is modeled by the four Work Stations in this model. Each Work Station corresponds to one of the activities that can take place at the real pill machine: setups for Aspirin A and B and production of Aspirin A and B. Hence, in the model we will have only one of these four Work Stations in operation at a time.

A Work Station in SimQuick can begin working if it has one of each of its input objects and no finished inventory in its internal buffer. When this model is started, no Work Station has any finished inventory and only Set Up A has each of its inputs (the one object in Signal and an object from Raw Material A). Hence, the model begins with Set Up A, taking these two objects and performing a simulated setup of the pill machine for making Aspirin A. Note that the "Output group size" of Raw Material A is 4. This means that the number of objects in Raw

Material A drops by four when one object is removed (this corresponds to 400 lbs of chemicals, which is the batch size for this scenario). When this setup is complete, Pill Machine A is the only Work Station with one of each of its inputs; hence, it begins to work (note that the one object taken from Set Up A still corresponds to the four objects originally taken from Raw Material A). The working time is taken from the table above. When Pill Machine A finishes working, it outputs four objects to Finished Pills A (the batch is broken back into its 100-lb components for departures) and one object to Set Up B. The object sent to Set Up B is a signal that Pill Machine A is done. With this signal, Set Up B now has both its input objects and can begin working. Note that when it takes one object from Raw Material B, the number of objects in Raw Material B drops by five. When this setup is complete, Pill Machine B begins to process a batch (again, the time is taken from the table above). When Pill Machine B finishes working, it outputs five objects to Finished Pills B (the batch is again broken up for departures). It also outputs one object to Signal, thus allowing the cycle to repeat. Observe that the sole reason for the Buffer Signal is to get the simulations going in the beginning.

Finally, during the simulation, pills leave the system via the two Exits according to the demand for each product. See Example 13 for an introduction to Exits. Note that we start the simulation with typical amounts of finished pills of each type.

Exercise 22: Simulate this process for 10 weeks (assume there are 8 working hours per day and 5 working days per week). Perform 100 simulations for each scenario. For each scenario, report the overall mean number of setups (this is given by the sum of the overall mean number of "Cycles started" at Set Up A and Set Up B), the overall mean inventory in each of the two finished pill storage areas, and the overall mean service level (at the Exits) for each product. Discuss how you would decide which batch size to use. (If you like, see Appendix 3 for how to use the feature Scenarios to run these model variations more efficiently.)

Example 23: A single-machine job shop

For this example, we build a model of a single machine in a job shop. The model can easily be extended to include multiple machines (up to the limitations of SimQuick). For example, in a factory, the machine could be a lathe, a drill, or a saw; in a service operation, it could represent an insurance claim check or a mortgage credit check.

The machine in this example processes four types of jobs. Arrivals of jobs are uncertain as are the processing times. They can be approximated by the SimQuick distributions in the following table (time units represent working hours; there are eight working hours per day). Processing times include the time for setting up the machine (which must be done before each job is started). Because each job is actually a batch, the processing times can be fairly long for some jobs. Once a job is started at the machine, it is finished before another job is started. The table also contains the lead time (number of hours between the arrival of the job and when it is finished) that is quoted to customers for each type of job.

Job	Time between arrivals	Processing time at machine	Quoted lead time
Job 1	Nor(13,3)	Nor(7,1)	16
Job 2	Nor(28,3)	Nor(8,1)	36
Job 3	Nor(32,3)	Nor(4,1)	24
Job 4	Nor(24,3)	Nor(3,1)	8

Management wants to compare two *priority rules* (which are used for deciding which job to do next at the machine):

Shortest Processing Time: When the machine finishes work on a job, it works next on the job that has the smallest (mean) processing time among the jobs that are ready to go.

Nearest Due Date: When the machine finishes work on a job, it works next on the job that has the smallest lead time among the jobs that are ready to go.

Modeling the process with SimQuick

A process flow map is provided below.

Process Flow Map for a Single-Machine Job Shop

The model works as follows. Jobs of type 1 arrive at Door 1, jobs of type 2 arrive at Door 2, and so on. Hence, the time between arrivals at each Entrance is the distribution given for the corresponding job type. After a job arrives, it goes into a Buffer for its type. The machine is modeled by the four Work Stations. The working time of each Work Station is the processing time given for the corresponding job type. Of course, when we run the model, we want only one Work Station to be working at a time. To accomplish this, we assign a common Resource, say R1, to each Work Station and make only one unit of this Resource available. (You may want to read Example 12 for an introduction to Resources.) A Work Station must have this Resource to work and, because there is only one unit available, only one Work Station can work at a time. When a Work Station finishes working on an object, the Resource becomes available. It is taken by the Work Station with highest Priority that has an input object ready to go. The Priority of a Work Station is simply determined by the number of its SimQuick table. For example, suppose during a simulation that the Work Station in table 1 finishes working on an object. If there is an input object for this Work Station, then it keeps the Resource and begins working on that object. Suppose there is no such object. If the Work Station in table 2 has an input object, it acquires the Resource and begins working on that object, and so on. Thus, to model the shortest processing time rule, we fill in the Work Station tables of SimQuick in the order WS4, WS3, WS1, WS2.

The Work Station tables for the shortest processing time model are provided below. Also provided is the Resource table (click on the "Resources" button on the Control Panel). It must be filled in so SimQuick knows how much of each Resource is available. (If we changed the 1 in this table to a 2, then two of the Work Stations in our model could work at the same time.)

Work Stations:

1

	Name →	WS4	
	Working time →	Nor(3,1)	
Output destination(s) ↓	# of output objects ↓	Resource name(s) ↓	Resource # units needed ↓
Finished Goods 4	1	R1	1

2

	Name →	WS3	
	Working time →	Nor(4,1)	
Output destination(s) ↓	# of output objects ↓	Resource name(s) ↓	Resource # units needed ↓
Finished Goods 3	1	R1	1

3

	Name →	WS1	
	Working time →	Nor(7,1)	
Output destination(s) ↓	# of output objects ↓	Resource name(s) ↓	Resource # units needed ↓
Finished Goods 1	1	R1	1

4

	Name →	WS2	
	Working time →	Nor(8,1)	
Output destination(s) ↓	# of output objects ↓	Resource name(s) ↓	Resource # units needed ↓
Finished Goods 2	1	R1	1

Resources:

Name ↓	Number available ↓
R1	1

Finally, we need to discuss how management decides between the two different Priority rules. We consider two performance measures for comparing the priority rules; they are expressed in terms of *flow time*. The *mean flow time of a job type* is the mean amount of time that type of job spends waiting plus being processed. The *tardiness of a job type* is zero if its mean flow time is less than or equal to its quoted lead time; otherwise, it's equal to:

(the mean flow time of the job type) – (the quoted lead time).

Management is interested in two performance measures:

The *overall mean flow time* is the mean of the mean flow times of each job type.

The *overall tardiness* is the mean of the tardinesses of each job type.

Exercise 23: For the job shop described above, run 100 simulations with each priority rule. Make sure the capacity of each Finished Goods Buffer is large enough; 100 will do the job. Management assumes that the demand patterns should remain stable for the next 100 days. For each rule, report the overall mean flow time and the overall tardiness.

Section 4: Quality and reliability in processes

In this section, we consider how to model two things in a factory that can go wrong. The first process involves quality problems with a product, and the second process involves reliability problems with a machine.

Example 24: A quality control station

Let's consider a simple process with a quality control station. Suppose we have an ample supply of raw materials, in this case, printed circuit boards. These boards are passed, one at a time, to a work station where a worker installs a few components. Each board is then passed to a quality control station where the installation is tested. Ninety percent of the boards pass this test and are then put into finished goods inventory. Those that fail the test are returned to the worker to be immediately examined and then retested. Management wants to know if investing in a new machine for the component installation would improve the throughput of the process. The new machine would have the same working time as the old machine, but the number of boards that pass inspection should increase to 95%. The remaining details are provided below.

Modeling the process with SimQuick

Here is a process flow map:

Process Flow Map for a Quality Control Station

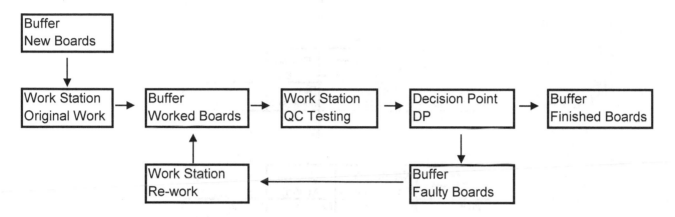

Observe that Original Work and Re-work are done at the same location in the factory by the same person. Hence, only one of these can be done at a time, so we assign a common Resource to them. We also want Re-work to have a higher Priority than Original Work. This means that if both Work Stations are ready to start working at some point in the simulation, then Re-work gets the Resource and starts working first. We instruct SimQuick to do this by entering Re-work into a table with a smaller number than Original Work. Hence, we have put Re-work into table 2 and Original Work into table 3, below. The effect of this is that whenever there is rework to be done, it is done before any new work is started. Here is how the SimQuick model looks (where time units represent minutes).

Buffers:

1	
Name →	New Boards
Capacity →	200
Initial # objects →	200
Output destination(s) ↓	Output group size ↓
Original Work	1

2	
Name →	Worked Boards
Capacity →	20
Initial # objects →	0
Output destination(s) ↓	Output group size ↓
QC Testing	1

3	
Name →	Faulty Boards
Capacity →	20
Initial # objects →	0
Output destination(s) ↓	Output group size ↓
Re-work	1

4	
Name →	Finished Boards
Capacity →	Unlimited
Initial # objects →	0
Output destination(s) ↓	Output group size ↓

Work Stations:

1			
Name →	QC Testing		
Working time →	Nor(3,.5)		
Output destination(s) ↓	# of output objects ↓	Resource name(s) ↓	Resource # units needed ↓
DP	1		

2			
Name →	Re-work		
Working time →	Nor(8,1)		
Output destination(s) ↓	# of output objects ↓	Resource name(s) ↓	Resource # units needed ↓
Worked Boards	1	R1	1

3			
Name →	Original Work		
Working time →	Nor(5,1)		
Output destination(s) ↓	# of output objects ↓	Resource name(s) ↓	Resource # units needed ↓
Worked Boards	1	R1	1

Decision Point:

1	
Name →	DP
Output destinations ↓	Percents ↓
Finished Boards	90
Faulty Boards	10

Note that we must also enter the one Resource into the Resource table and indicate there is only 1 available:

Name ↓	Number available ↓
R1	1

Exercise 24: Perform 100 simulations of an 8-hour work shift before and after the change. Report the overall mean <u>final</u> inventory of Finished Boards (i.e., the *throughput*) of the processes to assess the effect of the new machine.

Example 25: A machine with breakdowns

A factory has a metal stamping machine that is prone to breakdowns. Roughly 5% of the time, as the machine is being prepared for a new job, it gets jammed. Here is a process flow map of this situation using SimQuick elements:

Process Flow Map for a Machine with Breakdowns

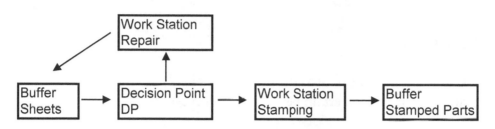

Objects representing the raw materials for this process are kept in the Buffer called Sheets. They next pass through a Decision Point where 95% of the time they go to the Work Station called Stamping and are processed as usual. However, 5% of the time they go to the Work Station called Repair. This corresponds to a breakdown of the stamping machine. We don't want any objects going to Stamping when this happens, so we assign a common resource to the two Work Stations. The working time at Stamping can be approximated by a normal distribution with a mean of 1 minute and a standard deviation of .1 minutes. The working time at Repair can be approximated by a normal distribution with a mean of 10 minutes and a standard deviation of 2 minutes. Note that objects that leave Repair go back to Sheets because they have not really been processed yet. (We assume they are not damaged.)

Exercise 25:

a.   Build a SimQuick model of the stamping machine process. Perform 100 simulation runs. Let time units represent minutes and run each simulation for 480 time units. Report the throughput (i.e., the overall mean <u>final</u> inventory in Stamped Parts).

b.   The factory is considering investing in a new stamping machine. The new machine is advertised as working at the same speed as the old machine but with 98% reliability. (Repairs should take about the same amount of time as for the old machine.) Using your model from part a, predict the throughput of the process using the new stamping machine.

Chapter 5: Project Management

Learning objectives:

- To model, simulate, and analyze projects with uncertain task durations.
- To understand the effect of uncertain task durations on estimates of a project's duration.

Overview

A project is a collection of tasks, with some sequencing requirements, that results in a single outcome. Projects are common in many businesses including construction, software development, and defense contracting. The modeling techniques of PERT and CPM are widely used for managing complex projects. A weakness of these models is that they typically do not incorporate uncertainty when estimating the duration of projects (or, if uncertainty is included in the model, it is not handled in a realistic fashion). In this section, we show how uncertainty can be incorporated in the PERT/CPM approach by viewing a project as a process and applying the techniques of process simulation.

Example 26: A software development project

We consider a (very) simplified project for developing a software product, which is graphically described below. Each box represents a task (or activity) that must be completed. A task cannot be started until all its predecessors (tasks to its left) have been completed. Management wants an estimate of how long the project is going to take.

A standard technique for addressing this problem begins by estimating the duration of each task (with a single number). The next step is to identify the sequence of tasks from beginning to end (e.g., Design Software, Develop Interface, Begin Phase 2, Test/Debug, Produce/Release) whose sum of estimated durations is a maximum; the so-called *critical path*. This largest sum is an estimate of the project's duration.

A Software Development Project

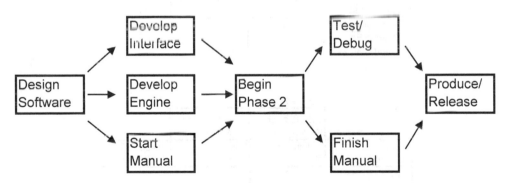

This technique does not capture an often crucial aspect of real projects; that is, task durations are typically uncertain and hence may not be modeled well by a single number. We propose to model projects with uncertain task durations using process simulation.

Modeling the process with SimQuick

The trick is to model each task with a Work Station. The arrows in the project diagram define the inputs and outputs of each Work Station in the usual fashion. The working times of each Work Station are statistical estimates of the corresponding tasks' durations. For this example, these estimates are provided in the following table, which is followed by our SimQuick model.

Tasks	Task durations (days)
Design Software	Nor(20,5)
Develop Interface	Nor(50,10)
Develop Engine	Nor(55,10)
Start Manual	Nor(20,5)
Begin Phase 2	Nor(2,.5)
Test/Debug	Nor(20,5)
Finish Manual	Nor(20,5)
Produce/Release	Nor(30,8)

Buffers:

1

Name →	Start
Capacity →	1
Initial # objects →	1
Output destination(s) ↓	Output group size ↓
Design Software	1

2

Name →	End
Capacity →	1
Initial # objects →	0
Output destination(s) ↓	Output group size ↓

Work Stations:

1

	Name →	Design Software	
	Working time →	Nor(20,5)	
Output destination(s) ↓	# of output objects ↓	Resource name(s) ↓	Resource # units needed ↓
Develop Interface	1		
Develop Engine	1		
Start Manual	1		

2

	Name →	Develop Interface	
	Working time →	Nor(50,10)	
Output destination(s) ↓	# of output objects ↓	Resource name(s) ↓	Resource # units needed ↓
Begin Phase 2	1		

3

	Name →	Develop Engine	
	Working time →	Nor(55,10)	
Output destination(s) ↓	# of output objects ↓	Resource name(s) ↓	Resource # units needed ↓
Begin Phase 2	1		

4

Name →	Start Manual		
Working time →	Nor(20,5)		
Output destination(s) ↓	# of output objects ↓	Resource name(s) ↓	Resource # units needed ↓
Begin Phase 2	1		

5

Name →	Begin Phase 2		
Working time →	Nor(2,.5)		
Output destination(s) ↓	# of output objects ↓	Resource name(s) ↓	Resource # units needed ↓
Test/Debug	1		
Finish Manual	1		

6

Name →	Test/Debug		
Working time →	Nor(20,5)		
Output destination(s) ↓	# of output objects ↓	Resource name(s) ↓	Resource # units needed ↓
Produce/Release	1		

7

Name →	Finish Manual		
Working time →	Nor(20,5)		
Output destination(s) ↓	# of output objects ↓	Resource name(s) ↓	Resource # units needed ↓
Produce/Release	1		

8

Name →	Produce/Release		
Working time →	Nor(30,8)		
Output destination(s) ↓	# of output objects ↓	Resource name(s) ↓	Resource # units needed ↓
End	1		

Observe that we have added Buffers at the ends of the process. The Buffer called Start contains a single initial object; its output is the first task of the project (in this case, Design Software). The Buffer called End has a single input from Produce/Release (and a capacity of 1). Thus we assume that the project has a single first task and a single final task. (Such tasks can be added with durations equal to zero, if they do not naturally occur in a project.)

The duration of the simulation is set to be some number of time units that exceeds the maximum possible duration of the project: in this case, 200 days. Let's run the simulation many times, say 500 times. Because the number of simulations is greater than 200, we must instruct SimQuick to report only the overall means for each simulation on the Results sheet. You instruct SimQuick to do this by clicking on the "Other Features" button followed by the "Hide Results Details" button.

Here is how the model works on our example. When a simulation begins, the object in Start immediately moves to Design Software. It stays there for an amount of time determined by our estimated duration of this task. After this, it is split into three objects, each of which goes to one of the outputs of Design Software. Each object stays at its Work Station according to our statistical estimate of these tasks' durations. Begin Phase 2 cannot start until it has one of each of its inputs; hence, it cannot start until each of its three predecessors is finished. The output of Phase 2 is two objects, each of which goes to one of its outputs. The same logic continues until Produce/Release sends one object to End.

Consider any one simulation. Throughout the simulation there is either 0 or 1 object in End. It follows that the mean inventory of End is the fraction of time during the simulation that the project is completed. If we average these numbers over all 500 simulations, we get the overall mean inventory of End. Using this we can estimate the duration of the project as follows:

Overall mean project duration = (1 – overall mean inventory of End) * (Simulation duration)

Exercise 26: Do the following for the software production example above:

a.   The duration of each task is described by a statistical distribution. If the duration of each task was precisely the mean of this distribution, what would the duration of the project be? (You do not need to use SimQuick, just find the longest total duration sequence of tasks from the beginning to the end of the project.)

b.   Report the overall mean duration of the project from 500 simulations of the above model (using the statistical distributions and SimQuick). How does this number compare with the duration reported in part a?

c.   Estimate the probability that the project will be completed in 150 days. You can do this by changing the duration of the simulations to 150 and reporting the overall mean final inventory in End.

Example 27: A house addition project

Consider the following house addition project:

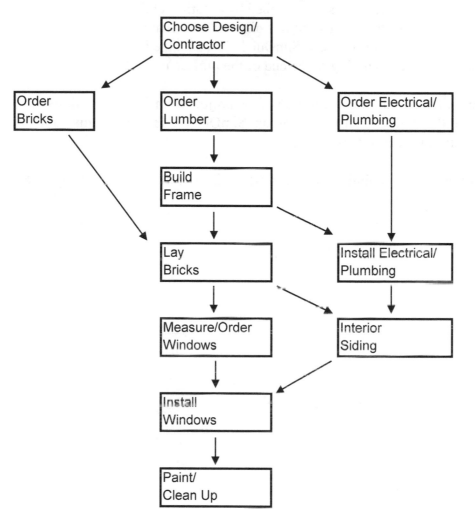

A House Addition Project

Tasks	Task durations (days)
Choose Design/Contractor	Nor(30,5)
Order Bricks	Exp(5)
Order Lumber	Exp(7)
Order Electrical/Plumbing	Exp(7)
Build Frame	Nor(2,.5)
Lay Bricks	Nor(2,.5)
Install Electrical/Plumbing	Nor(2,.5)
Measure/Order Windows	Exp(7)
Interior Siding	Nor(2,.5)

Install Windows	Nor(2,.5)
Paint/Clean Up	Nor(3,.5)

Exercise 27: Do the following for the house addition example above:

a.　The duration of each task is described by a statistical distribution. If the duration of each task was precisely the mean of this distribution, what would the duration of the project be? (You do not need to use SimQuick, just find the longest total duration sequence of tasks from the beginning to the end of the project.)

b.　Report the overall mean duration of the project from 500 simulations of the above model (using the statistical distributions and SimQuick). How does this number compare with the duration reported in part a?

c.　Estimate the probability that the project will be completed in 60 days. (See Exercise 26c for the method.)

Appendix 1:
The Steps in a Simulation Project

This appendix contains a checklist of the typical steps in a SimQuick simulation project.

Step 1: Identify the process to be studied and the objectives for improvement.

Step 2: Identify those aspects of the process to vary.

Step 3: Construct process flow maps of the existing process and the variations under consideration using the elements of SimQuick.

Step 4: Collect data needed for the SimQuick elements in the models.

Step 5: Choose SimQuick statistical distributions that best model the data. (Look at histograms of the data as discussed in Chapter 1, Section 3 and Example 11).

Step 6: Enter the model into SimQuick.

Step 7: Determine the duration of each simulation and how many simulations to run; enter into SimQuick.

Step 8: Run the simulations for the existing process. Check that the model is behaving like the real process. (This is called *validation.*)

Step 9: Run the simulations for the variations of the existing process.

Step 10: Analyze the results: Identify those variations that appear to have the best effects on the objectives. (This may require some statistical analysis; see Appendix 2.)

Appendix 2:
Enhancing SimQuick with Excel Features

In this appendix, we discuss several ways to take advantage of some basic features of Excel to enhance the power of SimQuick.

Creating process flow maps

Process flow maps can be created, for example, in Microsoft Word or Microsoft Excel using the built-in drawing features. This section contains a description of the method used for the figures in this booklet; it's quick and dirty but gets the job done.

Begin by inserting a new worksheet into the SimQuick workbook with which you're working. To do this, click on "Insert / Sheet" in the Excel menu. You can rename this new worksheet by double-clicking its tab at the bottom of the screen and typing a new name, say Flow Map.

Next, highlight any two cells, one above the other, in the new worksheet. On the menu, click on "Format / Format Cells." Then, click on the Border tab. Choose a wide line width and the outline option. Click OK. The two cells should now have a border. Highlight these two cells again and "Copy" them. Now highlight any two cells in the worksheet where you want to place an element in your process flow map and do a "Paste." Repeat this to place all the elements in your map. To move a box, just highlight it and drag it to a new location. Now you can label each of the boxes with the element type and name. Finally, from the menu select "Insert / Illustrations / Shapes," click on the arrow icon, and draw arrows between the boxes. (The details of these instructions will vary between different versions of Excel.)

Saving results

Suppose you have run a model and want to save some of the statistics from the Results worksheet. Copy any statistics from the Results worksheet that you want to keep and paste them into a new worksheet. Here is an example of a worksheet you might create for Example 1, the original bank:

	E	F	G	H	I	J
2	**Mean cycle times in teller line**					
3				**Simulation numbers**		
4		**1**	**2**	**3**	**4**	**5**
5	One teller, no machine	16.80	14.72	14.12	12.32	15.52
6	One teller, with machine	8.23	13.80	9.86	5.47	5.67
7						

You are now ready to perform some statistical analysis of these results using the statistical capabilities of Excel. Some examples are provided below.

Statistical analysis of SimQuick results

In this section, we consider several basic and important statistical calculations that can be performed on SimQuick outputs using the features of Excel. We assume the reader has had the equivalent of an introductory statistics course. Details on the Excel functions, statistics terminology (underlined below), and the related theory can be found many places online and in most introductory statistics texts. We will use spreadsheet formulas that became available in Excel for PCs in 2010 and Excel for Apple machines in 2011. These formulas have equivalent (or, in one case, near-equivalent) versions in earlier versions of Excel.

Let's discuss the data reported in the above table for the original one-teller bank model, Example 1 of Chapter 2. Consider the five output numbers for the "One teller, no machine" model: In the standard language of statistics, these numbers are a sample of size 5 taken from the (huge) population of all possible mean cycle times that SimQuick could produce for a single simulation of the process where the teller has no machine. Let's call this data as sample 1 and population 1. Similarly, the second row of 5 numbers is a sample, but from a different population: all possible mean cycle times that SimQuick could produce for simulations of the process where the teller has a machine. Let's call this data sample 2 and population 2.

One thing we would typically like to do is estimate the means of populations 1 and 2 by computing confidence intervals based on our samples. In order to do this we need to be able to compute sample means and sample standard deviations. SimQuick reports the sample means in its output (in the overall means column): 14.70 for the "one teller, no machine" case and 8.61 for the "one teller, with machine" case. These two numbers can also be computed for this example by typing the following two Excel functions into any two blank cells of the worksheet containing the above data: AVERAGE(F5:J5) and AVERAGE(F6:J6). The sample standard deviations can be computed for our two samples with the Excel functions: STDEV.S(F5:J5) and STDEV.S(F6:J6), which yield 1.67 and 3.43, respectively. Alternatively, by clicking on "Other Features," you can then click a button that instructs SimQuick to calculate sample standard deviations for you (whether or not you display the results details).

The margins of error for 95% confidence intervals can now be calculated with the Excel functions: CONFIDENCE.T(.05,1.67,5) and CONFIDENCE.T(.05,3.43,5), which yield 2.07 and 4.26, respectively. The interpretation of these numbers is that the mean of population 1 is in the interval 14.70 ± 2.07 with 95% probability; and the mean of population 2 is in the interval 8.61 ± 4.26 with 95% probability. The first number in the CONFIDENCE.T function is 1 minus the confidence level (i.e., 1 - .95); the second number is the sample standard deviation; and the third number is the sample size. Other commonly used confidence levels are 90% and 99%.

Confidence intervals tell us how accurately our simulation model is estimating various population means. Increasing the sample size (i.e., the number of simulations) tends to decrease the margin of error thus yielding better, more accurate, estimates. But increasing the sample size also tends to increase the running time of the model, so there is a trade-off to consider.

Another common statistical question to ask when doing process simulation is whether changing the model in some way results in a statistically significant improvement in some performance measure. In our above example, we may ask if the mean of population 2 is significantly less than the mean of population 1. This is done with a hypothesis test, which in this context is often called a t-test. To perform a t-test, we need a level of significance, which is an acceptable chance of error in our conclusions. Typical values for this are .01, .05, and .1; let's pick .05 for our example. We also need to make sure that our sample means exhibit the property we seek in the populations, namely that the mean for sample 2 is less than the mean for sample 1. Since this is true for our example, we can perform a t-test with the following Excel function: T.TEST(F5:J5,F6:J6,1,3), which yields .0063. The first two ranges in the formula refer to the two samples; the number 1 informs Excel that we want a 1-tailed test, and the 3 instructs Excel that our samples are taken from two independent populations that may have unequal variances. The number .0063 is called a p-value and since it's less than our significance level of .05, we can conclude that the mean of population 2 is less than the mean of population 1 (hence our process change resulted in an improvement in the cycle time) with at most a .05 probability of error.

Hence, if our model is a good one, then adding a check-reading machine in the real bank should significantly reduce the waiting time in the teller line. In general, the ability of the t-test to detect differences in population means will increase if you increase the number of simulations (i.e., the sample size).

Accelerating model entry

When entering a model into SimQuick that has several elements that are almost identical, use the ability of Excel to copy and paste ranges of cells. For example, consider Example 20, where we simulate a manufacturing cell. Here we enter six Work Stations whose SimQuick tables are quite similar. To ease this entry, enter the table for WS1, then copy the range B7:D11 and paste it into the cell G7; then repeat this for cells L7, Q7, V7, and finally AA7. The desired tables for WS2 through WS6 can then be obtained with minor editing. (Note that in SimQuick, a table can be copied and pasted only once, due to the way the pull-down lists work. However, you can paste more than one table at a time to speed things up. So, in this example, after pasting the first table into G7 and L7, you can copy the first three tables and paste that into the cell Q7.)

Appendix 3: Scenarios

In this appendix, we present a feature called *Scenarios*, which allows you to input, and then run, several variations on a given model, one after the other, with a single click on the "Run Simulations" button. Not only can this feature save you time, but the format of the Results allows for easy comparison of the model variations. We will illustrate this feature by revisiting Examples/Exercises 1, 9, 10, 13, and 14.

First, consider Exercise 1b, a variation on the original bank model. The exercise asks you to run several variations of the model, where the time between arrivals at the Entrance: Door is varied from Exp(2) to Exp(1.8) and so on, down to Exp(1.2). Using Scenarios, we can run these variations all at one time. To do this, fill in the SimQuick tables as before, except fill in the table for Entrance: Door as follows:

Entrance:

1	
Name →	Door
Time between arrivals →	ScenVar(1)
Num. objects per arrival →	1
Output destination(s) ↓	
Line	

Note that the time between arrivals has been changed to ScenVar(1). This function instructs SimQuick to find the time between arrivals by looking at column 1 in the table that can be viewed by clicking the button "Other Features" on the Control Panel and then "Scenarios." For this example, fill in the table as follows:

		1	2
	1	Exp(2)	
Scenarios	2	Exp(1.8)	
	3	Exp(1.6)	
	4	Exp(1.4)	
	5	Exp(1.2)	
	6		

Scenarios — Return to Contr — Scenario V

In general, this table can have multiple rows and columns filled in. Each entry in the table is one of SimQuick's statistical distributions (Nor, Exp, Uni, Constant, Dis, ChDist) or Cus or "Unavailable." Each row is called a Scenario and each column i corresponds to a Scenario Variable, which appears as ScenVar(i) somewhere in the input tables for the model. When you click "Run Simulations," SimQuick goes to the first row of this table, Scenario 1, and substitutes the entry in column 1 for each occurrence of ScenVar(1) in the model tables, substitutes the entry in column 2 (if there is one) for each occurrence of ScenVar(2), and so on. SimQuick then runs the number of simulations you specified on the Control Panel. SimQuick next goes to the second row of this table, Scenario 2, makes the new substitutions for the Scenario Variables indicated by this row, and reruns the model. When all the runs are completed, you can view the results for all the Scenarios by clicking "View Results."

Returning to our example above, the Scenarios table instructs SimQuick to run the model 5 times, first using Exp(2) for the time between arrivals of Door, then Exp(1.8), then Exp(1.6), and so on. After the "Run Simulation(s)" button is clicked, you can observe the Results displayed as follows (where we display here only the outputs for the Entrance: Door):

109

Simulation Results			Return to Control Panel				
Element types	Element names	Statistics	Scenarios (Overall Means)				
			1	2	3	4	5
Entrance(s)	Door	Objects entering process	58.99	66.73	76.68	85.06	96.06
		Objects unable to enter	0.00	0.08	0.23	0.59	4.66
		Service level	1.00	1.00	1.00	0.99	0.96

The column labeled 1 contains the overall means that would have been displayed by using Exp(2) for the time between arrivals. Column 2 contains the overall means that would have been displayed by using Exp(1.8) for the time between arrivals, and so on. The answer to the problem can be read off the row for the cycle times for Line (not shown).

Note: If your model has multiple Scenarios, and you are using Buffer Tracking for one or more Buffers, then the inventory levels reported on the Buffer Tracking worksheet are grouped by Scenario.

Let's next consider Example/Exercise 13, where we look at a periodic review inventory policy at a grocery store. The exercise asks you to run the model several times, where the capacity at the Buffer: Storage is varied from 70 to 94. To run these models at one time, using Scenarios, fill in the model as before, except fill in the tables for Buffer: Storage and Scenarios as follows:

Buffer:

1	
Name →	Storage
Capacity →	ScenVar(1)
Initial # objects →	0
Output destination(s) ↓	Output group size ↓
Purchase Requests	1

		Scenario Variables		
		1	2	3
Scenarios	1	70		
	2	74		
	3	78		
	4	82		
	5	86		
	6	90		
	7	94		
	8			

This table instructs SimQuick to run the model seven times, first using 70 for the capacity of Storage, then 74, then 78, and so on. Here are some of the Results (where we display only the outputs for the Entrance: Loading Dock):

Simulation Results			Return to Control Panel						
Element types	Element names	Statistics	Scenarios (Overall Means)						
			1	2	3	4	5	6	7
Entrance(s)	Loading Dock	Objects entering process	1041.30	1093.05	1137.19	1166.52	1187.83	1202.43	1213.74
		Objects unable to enter	1958.70	1906.95	1862.81	1833.48	1812.17	1797.57	1786.26
		Service level	0.35	0.36	0.38	0.39	0.40	0.40	0.40

For our third example, consider Exercise 14, which is an inventory process employing a reorder point policy. You are asked to consider several variations on the model where the values for the order size and the reorder point are changed. In order to simultaneously run the original model in Example 14 and all the variations in Exercise 14, fill in the SimQuick tables as follows:

Buffers:

1

Name →	Factory
Capacity →	1000
Initial # objects →	1000
Output destination(s) ↓	Output group size ↓
Delivery	ScenVar(1)

2

Name →	Reorder Point
Capacity →	ScenVar(2)
Initial # objects →	20
Output destination(s) ↓	Output group size ↓
Purchase Requests	1

Work Station:

	Name →	Delivery	
	Working time →	Nor(50,3)	
Output destination(s) ↓	# of output objects ↓	Resource name(s) ↓	Resource # units needed ↓
Reorder Point	ScenVar(1)		

Exit:

1

Name →	Purchase Requests
Time between departures →	Exp(2)
Num. objects per departure →	1

Scenarios		Return to Control Panel		
		Scenario Variables		
		1	2	3
Scenarios	1	35	20	
	2	35	25	
	3	45	25	
	4	55	25	
	5	65	25	
	6	75	25	
	7			

From the tables for the model, observe that ScenVar(1) occurs in two cells and ScenVar(2) occurs in one cell. From the Scenarios table, note that, during the first run of the model, the value for ScenVar(1) is 35 and the value for ScenVar(2) is 20, which are the values from the original model. For the second run the values are 35 and 25, respectively, and so on for the other Scenarios.

For a fourth example, consider the variation on the bank model introduced in Example/Exercise 9, which uses the "Unavailable" feature for Work Stations. The model is entered using an Entrance: Door; two Buffers: Line and Served Customers; and three Work Stations: Teller 1, Teller 2, and Teller 3. Fill in the tables for the model in the standard fashion, except enter ScenVar(1), ScenVar(2), ScenVar(3), respectively, for the working times at the three tellers. Then fill in the Scenarios table as follows:

Scenarios

Return to Control Panel

		Scenario Variables		
		1	2	3
Scenarios	1	Nor(2,.5)	Unavailable	Unavailable
	2	Nor(2,.5)	Nor(2,.5)	Unavailable
	3	Nor(2,.5)	Nor(2,.5)	Nor(2,.5)
	4			

Run the model as usual. Then you can observe in the Results the overall means for Scenario 1 (one teller), then Scenario 2 (two tellers), and finally Scenario 3 (three tellers), which should be essentially the same as you obtained in Exercise 9.

For a final example, consider the bank variation models in Example/Exercise 10, which uses the Changing Distributions feature. Enter the model into SimQuick with three tellers: Teller 1, Teller 2, and Teller 3. Fill in the tables in the usual fashion, except use ScenVar(1), ScenVar(2), and ScenVar(3) for the working times of the three tellers, respectively. Then the five model variations described in Exercise 10 can be run simultaneously by filling in the Scenarios table as follows:

Scenarios

Return to Control Panel

		Scenario Variables		
		1	2	3
Scenarios	1	ChDist(2)	Unavailable	Unavailable
	2	ChDist(2)	ChDist(3)	Unavailable
	3	ChDist(2)	ChDist(2)	Unavailable
	4	ChDist(2)	ChDist(2)	ChDist(3)
	5	ChDist(2)	ChDist(2)	ChDist(2)
	6			

112

Appendix 4: Custom Schedules

In this appendix, we present an example of a process that uses a SimQuick feature called Custom Schedules. This feature allows the user to input into SimQuick a specific schedule of arrivals at Entrances and departures at Exits; in general, this cannot be done using SimQuick's statistical distributions.

Consider the following variation on the linear flow process in Example 19.

Process Flow Map for a Linear Flow Process with Custom Schedules

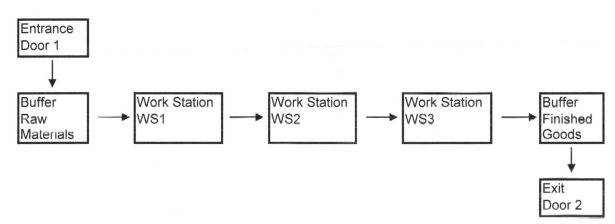

We let time units represent hours. There are 10 working hours per day and we want to simulate production for the next 100 days, so "Number of time units per simulation" is set to 1000. Some details are provided below.

Entrances:

1	
Name →	Door 1
Time between arrivals →	Cus(1)
Num. objects per arrival →	Cus(1)
Output destination(s) ↓	
Raw Materials	

Exits:

1	
Name →	Door 2
Time between departures →	Cus(2)
Num. objects per departure →	Cus(2)

Buffers:

1			2		
Name →	Raw Materials		**Name** →	Finished Goods	
Capacity →	Unlimited		Capacity →	Unlimited	
Initial # objects →	0		Initial # objects →	0	
Output destination(s) ↓	Output group size ↓		Output destination(s) ↓	Output group size ↓	
WS1	1		Door 2	1	

Work Station:

	1	
	Name →	WS1
	Working time →	Nor(5,1)
Output destination(s) ↓	# of output objects ↓	Resource name(s) ↓ / Resource # units needed ↓
WS2	1	

Custom Schedules:

1		2	
Times ↓	Quantity arriving/departing ↓	Times ↓	Quantity arriving/departing ↓
0	15	80	10
100	20	200	30
220	15	350	25
310	20	500	30
450	15	650	25
520	20	780	25
600	25	850	20
720	20	1000	10
850	10		
950	20		

Note that for the Entrance, "Time between arrivals" and the "Num. of objects per arrival" are filled in with "Cus(1)." This instructs SimQuick to look at Custom Schedules table 1 (shown above) for the arrival schedule. (To enter such a schedule, click on the "Other Features" button followed by the "Custom Schedules" button.) A different custom schedule table is used in this example to describe the departure schedule for the Exit.

Consider the Custom Schedule table 1 for Door 1. The table says that at time 0 (i.e., at the beginning of each simulation), 15 objects arrive at Door 1. Then at time 100, 20 more objects arrive, and so on. Table 2 for Door 2 says that at time 80, 10 objects (or as many as are available) can leave the process from Buffer: Finished Goods. Then, at time 200, 30 more objects can leave, and so on. Such specific schedules are impossible to describe using SimQuick's built-in statistical distributions and, typically, are used to describe arrivals and departures that have been worked out in advance, or are being considered, with suppliers and customers. In this case, running this model may help you to estimate how well the schedule for your customers will be met by the arrival schedule of raw materials (i.e., What is the service level at Door 2?). If the service level is too low, you may, for example, have to reschedule some of the arrivals of the raw materials.

Number in the "Times" columns should be numbers between 0 and the "Number of time units per simulation," and they should increase as you move down in the table. Each "Quantity arriving/departing" should be an integer between 1 and 10^{100}. A Custom Schedule can contain up to 1,000 rows.

Appendix 5: SimQuick Reference Manual

This appendix contains a concise description of the basic features of SimQuick for reference. SimQuick is an Excel-based software package for building simulation models of processes: waiting lines, supply chains, manufacturing facilities, and project scheduling. SimQuick is designed to be easy to learn and use, with clearly-defined functionality. The package has been used both to model real-world processes as well as in educational settings to introduce fundamental concepts of modeling, process simulation, and operations management.

SimQuick models consist of linked combinations of five basic *elements.* The element types are Entrances, Exits, Work Stations, Buffers, and Decision Points. *Objects* (representing people, manufactured parts, information, and so on) move between the elements, as dictated by links between them. You have a lot of discretion in how these elements are combined to build a model of a process. Characteristics of the elements are entered into SimQuick by filling in tables. Statistical distributions are a key characteristic; they capture the uncertainty inherent in almost all processes: arrival times of people at a service, times to process a document or machined part, demand for a product in a store, and so on.

The details of how to use SimQuick should be learned by reading the appropriate parts of the main text (especially, Chapter 1 and Example 1 in Chapter 2). The following quick tour through the various features of SimQuick makes references to the rest of text for more details. Comments are included for each button you can click on.

Installing and running SimQuick

SimQuick is a standard Excel file (with some macros). To use it you need only a basic installation of the spreadsheet Excel on a personal or networked computer. Please refer to Chapter 1, Section 4, or SimQuick.net, for details.

A free copy of SimQuick can be obtained at SimQuick.net.

SimQuick statistical distributions

A key feature of simulation software is a way to choose numbers randomly from statistical distributions. SimQuick provides the following functions for doing this.

Nor(m,s)   Numbers are chosen from a normal distribution with mean = m, standard deviation = s.

Uni(a,b)   Numbers are chosen from a uniform distribution between a and b, with a < b.

Exp(m)   Numbers are chosen from an exponential distribution with mean m.

Dis(i)   Numbers are chosen randomly from a discrete distribution described by filling in table i of the worksheet Discrete Distributions. (From the Control Panel, click on "Other Features" then "Discrete Distributions" to see the worksheet and tables.)

A fifth choice is simply a fixed number, referred to as a Constant.

More detail on the Nor, Uni, and Exp functions can be found in Chapter 1, Section 3. Discrete distributions are described in Example 11.

The numbers used in the above distributions must lie between 10^{-100} and 10^{100}.

These distributions are used for describing the working times at Work Stations, the arrival/departure schedules at Entrances/Exits, and the initial number of objects at Buffers. SimQuick also allows the arrival/departure schedules to be described with Custom Schedules (see Appendix 4). With this feature, schedules described by virtually any fixed numbers can be used.

The feature called Changing Distributions (inputted as ChDist(i)) allows a statistical distribution to change during the course of a simulation; for example, the arrival pattern of people at a service. This is discussed in Chapter 2 in Example 10.

The feature called Scenarios (inputted as ScenVar(i)) allows you to input, and then run, several variations on a given model, one after the other, with a single click on the "Run Simulations" button. This can save time entering model variations into SimQuick and allows convenient, side-by-side comparisons of output statistics. This is discussed in Appendix 3.

Many cells in the SimQuick tables have pull-down lists that indicate the various choices of statistical functions that are available. These choices vary somewhat from cell to cell.

Note: SimQuick is "case sensitive"; hence, the abbreviations used when inputting the distributions must use upper and lower case letters as indicated above.

Rules for all elements

As mentioned above, SimQuick models consist of linked combinations of five basic *elements*: Entrances, Exits, Work Stations, Buffers, and Decision Points. For each element in your model, you must fill in a table that describes the characteristics of that element. Each type of element has its own type of table. Blank tables can be found by clicking on the buttons on the Control Panel with the element names. When filling in tables, be sure to fill in table 1, then table 2, and so on, without leaving any blank tables between two filled-in tables. Fifty tables are provided for each type of element. The basic rules for the elements are given below.

Note: As mentioned above, SimQuick is "case sensitive"; hence, whenever a name for an element is entered into two or more places, it must be entered with the same upper- and lowercase letters. After the first time a name has been entered, it can then be selected from pull-down lists in other cells that contain names.

Entrances and Exits

Entrances are where objects enter the model and Exits are where objects leave the model. Entrances and Exits are introduced in Chapters 2 and 3, respectively. If your model has several types of objects entering (perhaps they follow different paths through a job shop or are combined on an assembly line), then you should have a separate Entrance for each type. The same holds if your model has several types of objects that leave; for example, if your model produces several different finished goods.

When filling in a table for an Entrance or an Exit, you must fill in the following cells:

1. *Name* (must be distinct from the names of other elements).
2. *Time between arrivals (departures)* and *Num. objects per arrival (departure)*. These two cells define the arrival/departure schedule for the objects that arrive/depart at this Entrance/Exit. The choices for both include the four SimQuick distributions and a number between 10^{-100} and 10^{100}.

    Other choices are a Scenario Variable (using ScenVar(i); see Appendix 3) and a Custom Schedule (using Cus(i); see Appendix 4). For time between arrivals, you can also use a Changing Distribution (using ChDist(i); see Example 10) or enter "Unavailable," which essentially removes the element from the model (see Example 9).

3. At least one *Output destination* (in the top row). This is a list of the elements to which objects at this Entrance are sent. Don't leave any blanks in the middle of the list.

If objects arrive at an Entrance during the simulation, then as many as will fit enter the model at that time. If there is not enough space for all of them, then those not entering are rejected from the model (and they cannot enter at a later time).

If objects are scheduled to depart from an Exit during a simulation, then as many as are available at that time at any of the inputs to the Exit will depart up to the specified num. objects per departure.

The following statistics are reported on the Results sheet for Entrances:

Objects entering process: This is the number of objects that arrived at the Entrance during the simulation and moved to one of its output destinations.

Objects unable to enter: This is the number of objects that arrived at the Entrance during the simulation but were unable to move to one of its output destinations (perhaps a Buffer was full or a Work Station was working at the time of arrival).

Service level: This is equal to $\dfrac{\text{Objects entering process}}{\text{Objects entering process} + \text{Objects unable to enter}}$.

The following statistics are reported on the Results sheet for Exits:

Objects leaving process: This is the number of objects that leave the model at the Exit during the simulation. (This typically represents filled demand.)

Object departures missed: This is the number of objects that could have left the model at the Exit during the simulation but did not because they were not available at the inputs to the Exit. (This typically represents unfilled demand.)

Service level: This is equal to $\dfrac{\text{Objects leaving process}}{\text{Objects leaving process} + \text{Object departures missed}}$.

Buffers

Buffers simply hold objects. Buffers are introduced in Chapter 2. When filling in a table for a Buffer, you must fill in the following cells:

1. *Name* (must be distinct from the names of other elements).
2. *Capacity.* This is the maximum number of objects that can be held at one time. It can be either an integer between 1 and 10^{100} or the word Unlimited (which is actually equal to 10^{100}).
3. *Initial # of objects.* This is the number of objects in the Buffer at the beginning of each simulation. It can be an integer between 0 and the capacity, one of the four SimQuick distributions, or a Scenario Variable.

The following are optional:

4. *Output destination(s).* This is a list of the elements to which objects at this Buffer are sent. If you fill in a row, you must fill in the top row. Don't leave any blanks in the middle of the list. The *Output group size* (an integer between 1 and 10^{100}) must be filled in for each output destination. This means that the Buffer groups together a specified number of objects before outputting them as a single object (e.g., if objects are put into boxes or sent to a machine as a batch). Hence, a Buffer will not send output to an element until it contains a number of objects equal to or greater than its group size.
5. *Track details?* If you enter "Yes" here, then, you are instructing SimQuick to keep track of the number of objects in the Buffer while the model is running. You can specify how many times to collect this number by clicking on "Other Features" and entering a number between 10 and 200 in the indicated cell. After running the model, you can click on "Other Features" and then "Buffer Tracking" to see the numbers collected. By entering a column number in cell D4 you can see a graph of the inventory level for the corresponding Buffer. The total number of Buffers being tracked times the number of Scenarios cannot exceed 250. See Example 8 for more details about Buffer Tracking.

If an output destination is not specified for a Buffer, then objects that enter the Buffer simply remain at the Buffer. Note that all objects entering a Buffer become indistinguishable. Hence, if you have two objects that represent different products, you probably shouldn't put them into the same Buffer.

The following statistics are reported on the Results sheet for Buffers:

Objects leaving: This is the number of objects that leave the Buffer and go to one of its output destinations during the simulation.

Final inventory: This is the number of objects in the Buffer at the end of the simulation.

Minimum inventory: This is the minimum number of objects in the Buffer during the simulation.

Maximum inventory: This is the maximum number of objects in the Buffer during the simulation.

Mean inventory: This is the mean number of objects in the Buffer during the simulation.

Mean cycle time: This is the mean amount of time that an object spends in the Buffer during a simulation. If no objects leave the Buffer during a simulation, then the mean cycle time is "Infinite."

Work Stations

Work is performed on the objects at Work Stations. Work Stations are introduced in Example 1 in Chapter 2. When filling in a table for a Work Station, the following cells must be filled in:

1. *Name* (must be distinct from the names of other elements).
2. *Working time.* This is the amount of work time per cycle. The choices are any one of the four SimQuick distributions or a number between 0 and 10^{100}. In addition, you can choose a Changing Distribution or a Scenario Variable. You can also choose to enter "Unavailable," which essentially removes the Work Station from the model. This can be used to easily add or remove Work Stations from a model, for example, when determining staffing levels.
3. *Output destination(s).* This is a list of the elements to which objects at this Work Station are sent. A Work Station must have at least one output destination. You must fill in the top row of the list; don't leave any blanks in the middle of the list. For each output destination, you must specify the *# of output objects* (an integer between 1 and 10^{100}). (Use this, for example, when a Work Station breaks or disassembles an input into a number of identical outputs; typically, this number is 1.)

The following is optional:

5.   *Resource names.* This is a list of the resources that this Work Station needs in order to work. For each name entered, you must also enter the *# of units* of this resource that is needed (an integer between 1 and 10^{100}). Each resource used must also be entered in the table accessed by clicking on the "Other Features" and "Resource(s)" buttons. Resources are introduced in Example 12.

When a Work Station finishes working on an object, it creates as many objects as designated for each output. Objects going to different outputs typically represent different things in the real process. If one type of output object is to be sent to any of several elements, then this one object type should be output to a single Buffer that then sends its outputs to these elements.

Work Stations retain output objects (in an internal buffer) until they have all been passed to subsequent elements in the model. A Work Station is *blocked* (i.e., it can perform no further work) until the created objects have all left the Work Station. Hence, for a Work Station to begin working, the following conditions must hold: the Work Station is not working; there is no finished inventory in the Work Station's internal buffer; there is one of each input object at each element providing the inputs; and, if resources are assigned to the Work Station, then the resources are available. When these conditions hold, the Work Station acquires one of each type of input object and the needed resources, determines the working time, and begins work. Resources are retained at the Work Station for the duration of the work; hence, they become unavailable to other Work Stations. When a work cycle is finished at a Work Station, its resources become available for reassignment.

Note that the requirement for a Work Station to have one of each input object before it starts working allows a Work Station to model (among other things) a machine whose job is to combine or assemble two or more objects.

The following statistics are reported on the Results sheet for Work Stations:

Final status: If the Work Station is working on an object at the end of the simulation, then its final status is "Working." Otherwise, its final status is "Not Working."

Final inventory (int. buff.): This is the number of finished objects in the internal buffer at the end of the simulation.

Mean inventory (int. buff.): This is the mean number of objects in the internal buffer during the simulation.

Mean cycle time (int. buff.): This is the mean amount of time an object spends in the internal buffer during a simulation. It does not include time spent working on the objects.

Work cycles started: This is the number of times during the simulation that the Work Station has begun working on a new set of inputs.

Fraction time working: This is the fraction of the time during the simulation that the Work Station is working on an object.

Fraction time blocked: This is the fraction of the time during the simulation that the Work Station is blocked.

Decision Points

Decision Points route objects to two or more (up to 10) outputs. Decision Points are introduced in Example 5. When filling in a table for a Decision Point, the following cells must be filled in:

1.   *Name* (must be distinct from the names of other elements).
2.   At least two *output destinations*: These are the elements to which objects at this Decision Point can be sent.
3.   An *output percentage* for each output destination: These numbers must be between 0 and 100 and must add up to 100.

When an object enters a Decision Point, it is randomly sent to one of the output destinations based on the percentages. A Decision Point requires zero time and has a capacity of one object. Hence, a Decision Point can be *blocked* (i.e., it will not route any additional objects) if the unit it holds cannot go to its output destination.

The following statistics are reported on the Results sheet for Decision Points:

Objects leaving: This is the number of objects that leave the Decision Point and go to one of its output destinations during the simulation.

Final inventory (int. buff.): This is the number of objects at the Decision Point (in its internal buffer) at the end of the simulation. The number can be 0 or 1.

Mean inventory (int. buff.): This is the mean number of objects in the internal buffer during a simulation.

Mean cycle time (int. buff.): This is the mean amount of time an object spends in the internal buffer during a simulation.

Simulation control parameters

To run a simulation, you need to specify two numbers on the Control Panel. First, you must enter the *Number of time units per simulation* (a number between 10^{-100} and 10^{100}). This determines how long each simulation runs. A good strategy is to first choose what time units in the model represent in the real world so the arrival/departure schedules and the working times are relatively small numbers compared with the Number of time units per simulation. Second, you need to specify the *Number of simulations* (an integer between 1 and 10,000). Because the numbers used in the simulation are generated randomly, you can get different results each time you run the simulations (unless you input a "seed," discussed below). Thus, you typically want to run multiple simulations and, perhaps, perform some statistical analysis of the results (see Appendix 2).

To perform the simulation(s)

Click the "Run Simulation(s)" button.

Running time

SimQuick can take a few minutes or longer to run if the number of time units per simulation is large, the number of simulations is large, and/or the number of elements is large. Running times will also depend on the speed of your computer. If SimQuick is not finished running after 30 seconds, a window appears and informs you of SimQuick's progress. In this case, you are given the option of stopping SimQuick or letting it continue. If you elect to have SimQuick continue, then you can specify a length of time. If SimQuick is not finished by this time, then this window reappears. SimQuick can be stopped while running at any time by hitting the Esc key.

Viewing the model

Click the "View Model" button to see copies of all the simulation control and element tables on a single worksheet. This sheet can be used to check the logic of the model and for printing the model. The model cannot be edited from this sheet.

Clearing the model

Clicking on the "Clear Model" button on the Control Panel clears all the SimQuick tables and the simulation control parameters.

Results and Results Details

Results of any simulation run can be obtained by clicking on the "View Results" button on the Control Panel. The first two columns contain the element types and names in the SimQuick model. In the third column, the types of statistics collected during the simulations appear. Slightly different statistics are collected for each type of element (and are discussed above). The statistics collected for each simulation appear in columns 4 and beyond. If the "Show Results Details" option has been chosen under "Other Features" and if the model has at most 200 simulations and at most one Scenario, then the details for each simulation are displayed in column 5 and beyond. The final location of every object that arrived at the model (or started at a Buffer) can be determined for each simulation, as well as how many objects passed through each element. Other summary statistics are also available, including statistics for Resources. If "Show Results Details" has been chosen, then each number in the column labeled "Overall means" is the mean of the numbers to its right. If "Hide Results Details" has been chosen, then only overall means are reported. In general, SimQuick will run faster if the "Hide" option is chosen. If a model has more than one Scenario, then only the overall means for each Scenario are reported. (For additional details, see "Rules for all elements" earlier in this appendix and Example 1.)

Other Features: Scenarios

See Appendix 3 for a detailed discussion of how to use Scenarios.

Other Features: Changing Distributions

See Example 10 for a detailed discussion of how to use Changing Distributions.

Other Features: Discrete Distributions

See Example 11 for a detailed discussion of how to use Discrete Distributions.

Other Features: Custom schedules

See Appendix 4 for a detailed description of how to use Custom Schedules.

Other Features: Optional random seed

If a number (from 1 to 32,000) is entered into the cell "Optional random seed" under "Other Features," then SimQuick generates the same sequence of random numbers each time it is run for a particular model. Hence the Results should be identical from one run to another. Note that the sequence of random numbers for a given seed may be different on different versions of Excel; in particular, between PCs and Apple computers. If this cell is blank, then SimQuick will generate different sequences of random numbers from one run to the next.

Other Features: Resources

Each resource that is used must be listed in the resources table, which can be accessed by clicking on the "Other Features" button on the Control Panel, followed by the "Resources" button. It is also necessary to enter the number (or amount) of each resource that is available (an integer between 1 and 10^{100}). Resources are assigned to Work Stations in the corresponding tables (the number needed must also be specified: an integer between 1 and 10^{100}). Resources are useful for modeling situations where one person is operating several machines, where a machine has several setup configurations, and so on. The "Mean number in use" of each resource during each simulation is provided on the Results sheet. This can be used to assess the *utilization* of resources. Resources are introduced in Example 12 and applied in Examples 20, 23, 24, and 25.

Other Features: Buffer Tracking

See the discussion of "Buffer Tracking" in this appendix under the discussion of Rules for all elements: Buffers. See also Example 8.

Other Features: Result details and Calculate sample st. dev.

See the discussion of "Result details" in this appendix under the discussion of Results and Results Details; and see the discussion of sample standard deviation in Appendix 2.

Additional model limits

At most, a model can have 250 elements, 10 outputs from an element, and 20 resources. (There is no additional restriction on the number of inputs to an element.) SimQuick provides 50 tables for each type of element.

How each simulation is performed

When a SimQuick simulation begins, a "simulation clock" starts in the computer and runs for the designated duration of the simulation. While this clock is running, a series of *simulation events* takes place at various times. There are three types of simulation events in SimQuick: the arrival of a shipment of objects at an Entrance, the departure of a shipment of objects from an Exit, and the completion of work at a Work Station. Whenever a simulation event occurs, the elements are scanned a number of times in the order of their *priority*: Entrances before Work Stations before Buffers before Decision Points before Exits; and, subject to this, in increasing order of table numbers.

No arrivals at an Entrance or departures from an Exit are allowed to occur when an Entrance or Exit, respectively, is "Unavailable." Also, no work begins at a Work Station that is "Unavailable." However, once a Work Station begins working on an object, it will finish that work even if it occurs during a time the Work Station has become "Unavailable."

A special purpose of the first scan of the elements in a model is to consider the resources: If a Work Station has just finished working, then its resources become available and its newly finished objects become available to subsequent elements. Resources are not reassigned until the second scan (hence, a high-priority Work Station may reacquire its resources immediately after completing work). After the first scan, elements attempt to "pull in" objects from their input elements (except for Entrances, which have no input elements). If a Buffer, Decision Point, or Exit has more than one input element, then it will attempt to pull in objects from its input elements in priority order. Methods for using the notion of Priority in modeling are discussed in Examples 12, 18, 23, 24, and 25.

CPSIA information can be obtained
at www.ICGtesting.com
Printed in the USA
BVHW021750220123
656846BV00012B/555

9 781518 857966